C000120156

Taking Flight
The Caged Bird

Taking Flight
The Caged Bird

One Woman's Story
of a Life Awakening

Liz Valloor

Ballpoint Press

*I dedicate this book to the memory of
Eddie and Annie Teresa Doherty, Drumhillock,
Gurteen, Co. Sligo, true soul friends who understood
that happiness is found in friendship and the ordinary*

Published in 2017 by Ballpoint Press
4 Wyndham Park, Bray, Co Wicklow, Republic of Ireland.
Telephone: 00353 86 821 7631
Email: ballpointpress1@gmail.com
Web: www.ballpointpress.ie

ISBN 978-0-9954793-2-6

© Copyright Elizabeth Valloor, 2017

All rights reserved. No part of this publication may be reproduced,
stored in a retrieval system, or in any form or by any means,
without the prior permission in writing of the publisher, nor be
otherwise circulated in any form of binding or cover other than that
in which it is published and without a similar condition including
this condition being imposed on the subsequent publisher.

While every effort has been made to ensure the accuracy of
all information contained in this book, neither the author
nor the publisher accepts liability for any errors or omissions made.

Book design and production by Joe Coyle Media&Design,
joecoyledesign@gmail.com

© Cover photograph by El Keegan

Printed and bound by GraphyCems

Contents

Acknowledgements

A VERY special thanks must go to my four wonderful children who inspired me to question my out of date beliefs about parenting and leadership.

To my friends who read the drafts and encouraged me to continue.

A special thanks to my sister Audrey Boss for her proof reading skills and the many suggestions.

To the children of Archbishop McQuaid N.S currently known as St. Columbanus N.S who challenged me to discover a more holistic approach to teaching.

To P.J. Cunningham, Ballpoint Press, for his patience and skills in helping me shape the book so that its purpose became clear and most of all to my beloved husband Francis Valloor who urged me to write it and without whom it wouldn't exist.

Thank you.

Awareness has set me free in ways unimaginable. The effort I put into trying to change others was frustrating and useless. The effort I put into changing myself was rewarding

Introduction

ONE night I stared at my bedroom wall and like Shirley in the film *Shirley Valentine*, I asked the question. "Is that all there is to my life?" I had become a human doing. With all my efforts I was truly unhappy.

In desperation, I sat in a church and wept from my soul. I had reached rock bottom. I handed the problem to God and declared that I was willing to see differently. I had nothing to lose.

Shortly afterwards, I was given a book called Awareness by Anthony de Mello S.J. He outlined three basic truths that made sense.

• You cannot make another person happy.
• You cannot make another person love you.
• You can only change yourself.

I discovered we all have scripts and we follow them as if they were real. I inherited mine from my parents and environment. Within my story were ideas, beliefs and habits that needed to be challenged. They were all stored in my subconscious mind. They came up for air in relationships and were especially noticeable when I was in difficulty.

I began the process of moving through fear and guilt as they emerged. This meant facing my biggest fear and that was disapproval. I had become an approval junkie. My body couldn't lie. It manifested in physical symptoms. My reactions showed me the truth.

Awareness has set me free in ways unimaginable. The effort I put into trying to change others was frustrating and useless. The effort I put into changing myself was rewarding. I could never access my potential or experience peace of mind if I had continued to follow my inherited script.

This book highlights through story how important it is to

heal. The pain we carry we unwittingly share with family, friends and colleagues. Happiness is the goal of life. As we let go of our pain, no one has the power to upset us unless we give them that power. The choice is ours.

In Search of Wisdom

'Smile, breathe and go slowly'
Thich Nhat Hanh

A LONELY, frosty, January day I walked the Sacred Hill of Tara in Co. Meath. I was feeling very low. I went there specifically to pray for some form of enlightenment on the meaning of my existence. I expected a good dollop of wisdom. As I walked over the frost covered earth, I could feel nothing but cold. I strolled down through the trees until I found my favourite spot. I prayed to be shown something that would help me.

It was getting late and the sun was going down. The expectation that I would find an answer diminished. No drama, no fantastic experience. Then it happened. A quiet whispering in my heart helped me understand that it's in the ordinary. It came like a knowing. What you seek is in the ordinary. Going outside myself would never bring me happiness. It is within.

What I was seeking would be shown to me in the moment, through relationships especially my relationship with myself.

My mind filtered information through my beliefs, ideas and experiences. My thinking had to go through that filter so that I could respond according to what I believed to be true

CHAPTER 1

The Awakening

'The mystery does not get clearer by repeating the question, nor is it bought by going to amazing places'
Rumi

' **M**OST people even though they don't know it are asleep. They're born asleep, live asleep, they marry in their sleep, they breed children in their sleep, and they die in their sleep without ever waking up. They never understand the loveliness and beauty of this thing they call human existence." (Awareness Anthony de Mello)

I read this piece in May 1994. Our thinking, according to Anthony de Mello, has no basis in reality. It is because of our programming, our personal scripts. He likened our minds to computers. No business could operate on Windows 98 in 2016. Why do we expect our current relationships to be successful, operating on outdated beliefs? It was only when I allowed my mind to open to experience a more liberating programme, did I begin to change.

My mind filtered information through my beliefs, ideas and experiences. My thinking had to go through that filter so that I could respond according to what I believed to be true. If we were ever to experience true happiness, de Mello demanded that we question all beliefs, but especially those that elicited a powerful response in us.

I was struggling to make sense of my unhappiness. The more effort I put into my relationships the more complicated they became. I wanted to make people happy. I wanted them to love me. I wanted them to change so that I could be happy. He likened us to puppets: praise us and we are upbeat, criticise us and we are down. That was true for me.

"Drop all your ideas, beliefs and attachments. Empty your mind of all that went before!" "Seeing," he said, "is the most arduous work we would ever do." I could not empty what I could not even see. It's not possible to heal cancer when you do not know it exists. I had to be prepared to let go all unhelpful thought patterns handed down through the generations that were unhelpful. He asked me to, at the very least, look at them and see if any of them was of benefit to me. For me looking was insufficient. I needed the courage to follow through and I didn't have it then. Life appeared to be simpler blaming others for my unhappiness. To accept that the quality of my relationships mirrored my own state of mind was a difficult pill to swallow. I believed until then that I had total responsibility for the happiness of my family. My heart was telling me to do everything I could to make them happy. What I didn't realise was that my heart was responding to my own brokenness, not to theirs. Unhappy people control!

In reality, did any of my efforts make them happy? I didn't know the secret to the peace I longed for was within my own heart and even if I was told at that time, I would have thought that it was too simplistic.

Previously I never questioned the validity of my beliefs. I accepted my way of thinking as being the truth. Faith and belief, he said, are two different things. Faith based on personal experience is not easily threatened by opposing beliefs. Unquestioned beliefs are problematic. When opposing beliefs threatened mine I became anxious and defensive.

Truth hits you hard! You can reject it and refuse to acknowledge it but it comes back to you time and again through different happenings. I was becoming more aware of how I related through fear and guilt and a need to control my environment.

I wanted my children to be safe, healthy and successful, but my helicopter mothering was actually creating a situation that was unsafe for them. I was being prompted to open my eyes to a different perception and I was frightened of letting go.

I was prepared to at least question my beliefs and see where they came from! What had I to lose!

How I perceive a situation is not how another might perceive it. My thinking is based on my experiences and beliefs, while another person's is based on theirs. Reality is not the problem, our response to reality is.

*Instead, observe the
reactions in your body
and the feelings that arise!
They will disclose you to yourself*

CHAPTER 2

Reflection

'Every relationship recreates the original relationship.
The discovery of love is a re-discovery'
Sigmund Freud

S HE burst through the door like a tornado. "Is this anything to do with religion?" She demanded. "No, it hasn't." "Is this about Reiki?" "No, it isn't." She chose the seat in front of me, sat down with a thud, breathing heavily. There was immediate silence in the room.

I outlined what we would be covering over the ten weeks and began with a meditation. She slugged water noisily throughout the meditation and slammed the water bottle on the table. The tension in the room increased. I asked if the group would refrain from taking notes. I said that note taking is like reading subtitles. Your attention is divided if you take notes. Instead, observe the reactions in your body and the feelings that arise! They will disclose you to yourself. Her face went red with anger though she didn't say anything.

We had a coffee break. She didn't join us. I wondered if she had enough of my awareness teaching and left the building. I was settling in to begin again when she came through the door, sat down and bellowed, "You will not tell me what to do. I will take notes if I want to take notes. I didn't come to a course to be told what to do." I waited until her energy dissipated. I took a deep breath before speaking. "What was your relationship with your mother like?" I asked. This time I thought she would lunge forward and choke me. "What has my mother got to do with this?" she belched out at me. "This is important," I replied, "otherwise I would not ask you." She said, "She was constantly at me, telling me what to do. She never stopped criticising me."

"What is happening here is that you are projecting your relationship with your mother on to me. I am not your mother and I am not criticising you," I assured her. "I am only saying that if you could desist from note taking and observe your body as I speak, you will be able to see the effect of what I say more clearly. You will understand much more through observation. Any woman in authority will probably bring up these feelings in you." She went silent. When the talk ended she slipped away quietly.

I sat in my car that night and wondered how I came to a point where I was not disturbed by what had happened. Previously I would have been the first in the stampede towards the nearest exit. At what point did I let go of fear in relationships?

Anthony de Mello said, "Even if you practise awareness for three weeks you will see a difference." I had been practising for some years. This lady was my gift. She clearly showed me how far I had moved from the little mouse I used to be and that in order to be strong I didn't need to become aggressive. I hoped I was her gift.

The hurt from our initial relationships is played out over and over again in our current relationships until we heal that hurt. Our fear of confronting it, is our biggest obstacle.

CHAPTER 3

The Influence of Family Values

'You cannot make another person love you'

Anthony de Mello

M Y arrival into the world was greeted by a letter of condolence from my grandmother. Nothing unusual in this, her expression of concern was in direct correlation to family values and beliefs that were particular to her time and place. I was born the fourth girl on a farm that had been in the family for generations. Who would continue the family line was uppermost in her mind and I know my parents felt the same.

My father's ancestors leased land from the Rothwells, the local Anglo-Irish landlord. Ultimately with the passing of the Land Acts in the early years of the 20th century, they were able to buy the property. This allowed them become what he termed gentlemen farmers. My mother's ancestors were Protestant and Anglo Irish. Her grandmother married a Catholic. My mother felt that she had come from landed gentry. She would refer to them as Old Money and played out this role in her mind throughout her life.

My birth was a significant event. She would have felt she had failed in some way. I knew instinctively that being born female was not something to celebrate. The effect of this underlying current was that I continuously tried to justify my existence. I wanted to be appreciated like the boys who were born subsequently, and developed behaviours to compensate. I became the tomboy.

My paternal grandmother visited regularly in those early years. Holding on to her beliefs made it difficult for her to relate to me. Each morning my brother and I were sent up to say good morning to her. I hated it. My relationship to her was already tainted, that was clear. I overheard her say to my mother, "I just can't stand that child." I felt deeply hurt. I had no idea what I had done to create this feeling in her but the impact of this left me with my first feeling of not being good enough and not being equal in relation to my brothers. It put words on what I sensed. "What was there to love in me?" There was something wrong with me!

The absorption of another's values had begun. The feeling went into my memory bank and stayed there for forty years until it became impossible to ignore it. This is not to blame her or my parents. It is important to understand our early years from an adult's perspective but as long as we hang on to our feelings of hurt and shame we continue to view the present through the eyes of that little child. That I was not acceptable to my grandmother really had nothing to do with me but I believed it had. I blamed her for my feelings of not measuring up. I was only a child but if I continued throughout my life to hold on to that initial perception then that had everything to do with me. How do we imagine we can lead independent lives if we have no knowledge of the filters that control our perceptions? These filters, our lenses of perception have been placed there by our experiences. We operate out of that lens. Then, with authority we proceed to plonk that perception onto the next generation without discernment.

No adult challenged my grandmother's authority. This was a very powerful message to a young child. My youngest brother declared to her at the dinner table, "You are not the order man around here." I secretly admired him for it. We had no role models for a healthy relationship with authority. My mother and father never openly dealt with challenges from authority figures. The clear message was that you had no power over authority, you had no right to challenge it and if you did you would be blamed for the discord. Guilt is a powerful manipulator!

Blame leaves us with a sense of helplessness and resentment. We give our power to those we blame. The biggest problem with the blame game is that everyone loses.

CHAPTER 4

Initiation into the School System

'The greatest danger for most of us is not that our aim is too high and we miss it, but that our aim is too low and we reach it'

Michelangelo

T HE evening before my first day at school I see myself sitting on a blue wicker stool in the bathroom. I had reached my fifth birthday. My mother was doing her best to make me respectable for the occasion.

It was a two teacher, basic, national school and I have no lingering bad memories of that early experience. The juniors were in one room, the centre of the building was for the Master Mr. Crowley and his family and the other room was for the seniors. Dry wooden toilets outside with a smell of Jeyes fluid disinfectant! Squares of newspaper hanging on the wall with a sign "Only to Be Used When Necessary!"

We brought turf to be used in the fire in the centre of the room and on a small primus stove the teacher made cocoa for the children. The teacher, Ms. Smith, seemed ancient to me. She arrived on her black Nelly bicycle each day. In that small room we learned how to read, write and do mathematics. There were inkwells built into the desks. I loved those old pens and the feeling of blotting paper. Great attention was given to the art of handwriting. We learned to knit socks, mittens and sew French knots for embroidery, blanket stitch and darning.

As Fr. James Patrick Hederman OSB said in his book "The Boy in the Bubble", "The great dilemma for those of us involved in education, is that we are trying to prepare our children for a world that we will never know and can never enter. Every generation is a new world never before explored by humankind. And yet we have to prepare those who are destined to inhabit this new territory for the task ahead of them." Well! Darning socks and blanket stitch was never going to be part of my world! After our First Communion we were moved to the other side of the school to the Master. He did have a stick and used it from time to time but I do not remember him being malicious. He was kindly by nature, inclined to be a bit eccentric and fond of the odd drop or two of whiskey.

I never experienced fear of learning in that small country school. I neither felt intelligent nor unintelligent. It was as it was! There was something very human about The Master. It was this aspect I missed most when I was moved to the convent school. I never felt that effortless relationship to learning again because my initial immersion into convent school education was traumatic.

At home there was no discussion about change of school. I was told I was moving with my sister. I was aged nine. We met with the head nun and she gave us a few tests. She tut tutted about our lack of skills and recommended we go for extra tuition. My sister and I felt there was something wrong with us. For the first time we were aware of learning expectations, we began to feel that perhaps we were stupid. This shattered my confidence.

I was friendly with Maura, the Master's daughter in Girley National School. We always played together but when I changed schools he became extremely upset and wouldn't allow the friendship continue. There are always consequences to actions. Adults incapable of communicating concerns are inclined to take their frustration to the lowest rung in the ladder. I doubt my parents approached him or he them. I doubt they understood the emotional consequences for my sister and me.

In the new school I found it very difficult to make friends. It was a case of town mouse and country mouse. I had a sense of identity in my country school but was absolutely lost in the town. At playtime I stood by the wall. Classmates knew each other for years and had established friendships. My feeling of inadequacy because of having to go for extra tuition and my fear of not being able to rote learn was the end of fun. Learning was now something different. Sixth class was the worst and though I was never beaten, seeing others, especially children from the poorer areas of the town being beaten sickened me. You learned quickly to be quiet but no matter how you tried, it was not possible to escape the waspish remarks. Unhappy people spread their unhappiness freely and bless that nun she spread hers like snuff at a wake.

I remember the nun telling some inane joke. One of the wags in the class said "Tickle me and I'll laugh," to her friend. The nun overheard the remark and demanded she repeat it so that the whole class could be a witness to her folly. She was boiling with rage. The girl repeated what she said and her pal giggled. The nun demanded she come up to the top of the class and get down on her knees. I think it took more out of me watching the spectacle than it did out of the girl in question. She would live to see another day! The friend's turn was next. She got down on her knees but as soon as the spindle came near her she pulled her hand away begging, "Don't bate me sister." The whole thing was turning into a farce because this girl was capable of putting on a good show. "Sister, sister, don't bate me," she continued.

Though I never experienced a beating, the fear of ever stepping out of line and the fear of authority had a long lasting effect. Instituting fear in children could never make a society able to face the challenges of life in a healthy manner. I lived within the constraints of fear, fear of authority, lack of questioning, guilt, until ultimately I began to change. The experience of this way of teaching propelled me to discover new ways of dealing with behaviour in later years but also showed clearly that fear could never create educated, free thinking, responsible people. Fear of failure and ridicule, led to a fear of taking risks, and encouraged obedience and conformity. Fear of ridicule, meant it was very difficult for me to voice an opinion or even take a chance to form one.

One comment a nun made spurred me on, "Go home and feed the cows and the pigs and whatever you have on that farm because that is all you are fit for." She smirked when she had finished and looked to the class for approval. She propelled me to prove her wrong. I was determined to do well. I didn't respond, I just stomached it. Unfortunately, I needed that type of impetus to make me go the extra mile, to show my capability. There was no freedom in that! Avoidance of conflict is a skill learned and I was its best pupil. Silence is seen as being inactive. It is not. Not doing or saying is also an action.

I did love cooking and we had a class every Tuesday. We cooked lamb stew, scones and brown bread. I happened to be beside a girl who had a reputation for forgetfulness and giddiness. This day we were making brown bread. We had completed the task and were preparing to put the uncooked bread on to trays when Mary saw to her horror that she had forgotten to put in the bread soda. This meant that her bread would not rise and it was certain that she would be in for a chastisement from the nun. She grabbed her tray quickly and pushed the bread soda into the dough with her fingers. There were glass ovens in the cookery hall and we were invited to look at the progress. The nun spotted Mary's flat offering. With a swish of her tea cloth she opened the oven door, took out the offending cake of bread and demanded to know the owner immediately. Mary had to own up and with bowed head took the dutiful lashing of words. I felt so sad for her and the usual feelings of anxiety took over. What I hadn't reckoned on was Mary's reaction when she left the hall. She laughed heartily. It had absolutely no effect on her. It turned her into a celebrity. What is interesting to me is how this incident that was not even directed at me should affect me, and Mary, who to me was humiliated, was not in the least bothered. Anthony de Mello's point that the problem is inside us is correct. If we are reacting, then we have a problem. Mary's take on the situation was completely different from mine. I was a cowering mess and she was Queen of the class.

I was looking at the situation through my filter. Mine was a fight or flight situation. She enjoyed the drama.

Fear was my permanent resident. I masked it well!

The problem is inside us. Our reactions highlight this truth. Check out the source of the reaction. Small changes in our thinking is our path to freedom.

When you are brought up on a diet that the other person's happiness is dependent on you, and that you are solely responsible for any discord, it is not easy to say 'no'

CHAPTER 5

Growing Pains!

**'You cannot make another person happy,
something has to change in them'**
Anthony de Mello

M Y maternal grandfather George was an important influence in my life. As a child I was allowed to visit him and my grandmother with my brother. Grandad lived at Mount Thunder Stud. He was very different from anyone we knew. He was quiet, read books and smoked a pipe. There was a contentment about him that we all sensed.

One day while we were on holidays with him, Grandad brought my brother and me down to Leixlip village to get the daily newspaper. He put us into the back of his blue van that he referred to as 'The Bentley.' While there, he bought us two lollipops in Mrs. Jacobs' shop. The counter was so high we couldn't see across it but she brought down the jars to let us choose. We weren't allowed eat them until we got home.

We were sitting on a white fence eating our lollipops as Grandad walked the horses in a circle, when my brother began to cry. He had swallowed his. I felt so sorry for him that I bit through mine and ate it quickly. The moment mine was finished he produced his from under his tongue. I was very upset that he should do that to me. I was easily manipulated.

I had little discernment in my giving even then. My giving was generally guilt related, an inability to say no. It didn't make for good relationships. When you are brought up on a diet that the other person's happiness is dependent on you, and that you are solely responsible for any discord, it is not easy to say no. What I was never told was that not giving in certain circumstances could actually be more beneficial to the one who wishes to receive on demand.

Grandad's relationship to Religion was refreshing. To him a grown man running to a priest for confession was infantile. If you needed someone to forgive you without reflection on your own behaviours then it was useless. A system that needed an angry father like figure to put manners on you once a month or year was stupidity at its best. Where was personal responsibility? The seeds for questioning my understanding of religion were planted here.

Disappointment surrounding my birth meant that I craved love and acceptance. When praised it was like being accepted by my father or mother, when criticised even if it was constructive and loving, brought a torrent of tears. I was a puppet. Praise me and I felt validated, criticise me and I was devastated. I thought that was normal. The craving for acceptance and love limited my ability to think on my own, to form opinions without fear and to question. So much energy went into keeping up appearances and worrying, that there was little space for creative thinking. The ability to communicate freely was very limited as I was apprehensive of a backlash. I was blind to what this did to my mental and physical health.

As Meister Eckhart put it, "It is not by your actions that you will be saved but by your being." It is not by what you do but by who you are! I needed to find that person behind the hurt feelings.

When I was about thirteen years old I went on another holiday to Grandad. I can't remember doing anything extremely exciting other than playing with my friend Ann who lived on a farm nearby, but that nurturing time held me. At the end of the holiday Grandad gave me a ten-shilling note." Promise me that you will not spend this on anyone but yourself." I thought that would be selfish and immediately went down to the village and bought gifts. He wouldn't have had a problem if I had been able to retain something for myself. The problem was that I gave everything I had.

He came to live with us when I was fourteen years old. He hadn't planned on staying long as doctors told him he had only six months to live. He was to be with us for ten years. Grandad introduced me to a world of books, the local library, the Librarian Molly Kelly, and taught me how to drive his car. Every week he gave me pocket money. This was unheard of in my family.

Each school holiday there was what was referred to as a hop in the local golf club. It would be a disco in today's terms. I needed a new dress. I thought to ask Grandad for the money. He asked how much did I need. I told him, and he said, "You can have it but your pocket money will be stopped for ten weeks until it is paid for." He wrote the date of my return to pocket money on the packet of his razor blades. I didn't feel demeaned but I understood it had to be something important before I asked again. I also made sure that the dress I bought was worth it. I never took him for granted again. He checked the behaviour without diminishing me.

As a young teenager I began to push the boundaries of authority. Sitting in our dining room one Thursday night watching Top of the Pops I told my father to stop rattling his newspaper. The Beatles were singing A Hard Day's Night and I couldn't hear it from our black and white television. Whereas this would have warranted a clout around the ear any other time, he was so shocked that he said, "I don't know what the world is coming to, when a man can't read his paper in his own home." If I could have learned from this incident it would have been the lesson that it is possible to challenge. It's how you challenge that is important.

At sixteen I went to Dublin during the summer holidays to mind children. This was quite normal then. The first three girls were sent to work during the summer months. They called it au-pairing. I hated it. I had been used to the countryside and I felt totally confined. From the comfort of my home I thought I was off to have adventures only to find when I got there I was terrified. I had very little money. Sunday was a no cooking day in that first house and we had salad. I was used to food being plentiful and proper meat at home. Potatoes were counted as they went into a pot. Sacrilege! I considered life in Dublin as a form of war rationing.

When I needed to get away from everyone at home I took to the fields. It cleared my head and gave me space from immediate family. In Dublin I felt confined like an animal in the zoo. I crash landed. I was lonely and miserable. My only contact was an aging, eccentric spinster Aunt - Aunty Bea, who lived in a rambling house in Upper Leeson St. Her presence and curled up egg sandwiches was better than nothing. During this time as au pair, my limited communication skills presented themselves. I feared asking could I make a phone call. I waited for them to acknowledge my needs. It didn't happen. I couldn't wait to go home.

I went home at the end of August with a sense of relief and a polite accent that drove my mother crazy. September I got the results of my Intermediate exam and I had done very well. My Dad was proud as a peacock and took me out for a meal in The Park Hotel in Virginia. There was some value in having girls after all. Having succeeded in the Intermediate exam, I felt I had an anchoring point. It really did build up my self-esteem. Evidence of a brain!

My mother's reaction was very different. She told me to be quiet as I was upsetting everyone. I was shocked. I imagined she would have been the one to be excited, not my father. I was really upset then but now understand that it was the beginning of her seeing that her life was slipping away and her talents were not going to get much of an airing. We were, as girls finding an escape and she was left with unrealised dreams. She was only nineteen when she got married after the war in 1945 and by 1966 she was forty with nine living children. It puts a different perspective on it now, as I see how it must have been for this beautiful, talented, young woman. We share our misery freely when we feel we are trapped and our life is being whittled away! We don't mean to but we do. I needed to heal my misery or I would have done the exact same.

My father controlled finance making every penny a prisoner. Requesting money was like asking for hen's teeth. If there was resistance to the request, even the slightest hesitation would make me squirm. Internally I said "I would sooner scrub floors than ask you for money." That attitude was the training ground for me taking on too much responsibility around finances later on. Mortification around money completely controlled me. I could see me in front of him asking for money. He would win an Oscar for his performance. "Squeeze, squeeze, squeeze like a sponge. I will end up in the poor house with the lot of you." His behaviour had the desired effect. That feeling of being belittled had a powerful impact on me. The nearest I can get to describing my father, even in gesture and habits would be to say he was like the actor Tony Doyle in John McGahern's drama Amongst Women. Down to the way he put the hat on his head was the same. Seeing Amongst Women on the television placed him in Irish Society. He was not alone in his thinking. He was part of a social order in a changing Ireland and he responded to change as best he could over the years.

The ability to pretend I did not care increased as the years went by. I opened a cupboard in my heart, locked in the pain and resentment and threw away the key until age forty-two. Peace for peace sake was a mantra in our household growing up. Anything for a quiet life! My mother was always afraid of rocking the boat as she would put it and always ended with the remark, "It is all right for you lot to stir up trouble and then leave me to deal with it." I loved her with a passion and did not want to do that to her. This silenced me.

Within such a system you had to find a way to be heard, to be acknowledged as good. I did not voice what I was thinking or feeling. Many times I was told, "Liz won't mind." Liz did mind but didn't say anything. I gave the appearance of not caring. It was a lie. I did care. I tried to give the impression of being powerfully independent. Peace for peace sake comes at a heavy price. Pent up frustrations would surface eventually. My staying silent on matters important to me, meant that the other gained power. I was giving them mine! To become strong, I had to befriend my weakness so that it would no longer control me. You cannot move forward unless you understand what controls you.

The following summer I was sent to another family. This was a much different experience. I was treated as a member of the family and it made my time there very enjoyable. I was there to help John and Pat with their two daughters Hilary and Patricia. After a few weeks we went on a holiday to Lough Rynn in Co. Leitrim. As I had only ever gone to my Grandad's this was something new for me. It was then owned by a struggling aristocrat, now it is a top class hotel.

John and Pat rented a house on the estate and it seemed huge to me. It was surrounded by a lake and we went boating whenever we liked. The farmyard was nearby and I used to go down and get milk from the farmer. I was in my element as I was familiar with the set up. I still see us dive from the boat, swim and picnic by the lake. The weather made up for it too. As we were mooring the boat John got out and began sinking in the sand. "Quicksand," he roared. He was actually serious. Where in Leitrim would you get quicksand? I laughed until I pained. He was not impressed at my irreverence. The difference being that I was not afraid to laugh nor did I feel that he would reprimand me. In this environment I was beginning to blossom.

I returned home to begin studying for my Leaving Certificate. Whereas I didn't have a care in the world, the pending exams and the knowledge that I had to be out of the house permanently within a year brought its own pressure. Staying at home was not an option. You imagine you can do it differently, you think you have all the skills necessary but the reality that you have to pass exams and find your way in the world without help is overwhelming when you are very young and with no mentoring. There was no Guidance Counselling and only a set number of jobs mentioned over the course of the years. I could either be a nurse, teacher, bank official, civil servant or enter some insurance company. Nurse and teacher were out because that would have needed money for fees over a prolonged period. I had no idea of my talents and even if I had been guided in their direction they would not have been cool enough for the heady 1960's. The Beatles were in full swing, mini-skirts and long blond straight hair were in. Lulu, Cilla and Sandy Shaw were my idols. I felt awkward, stupid, shy and powerful in equal measure. I was also what my next door neighbour would say "inclined to be a bit plump." She knew how to bring me down to size. She never minced words. I rode my bicycle into the local town to get my hair cut. On the way back my only mission was to get past her house without a comment. Just when I thought I was successful her head popped up over the hedge and if she had been playing darts she would have hit a bull's eye. "Run into a combine harvester, did ya?" she shouted. I had just cut my hair short like Twiggy, who was all the rage at the time. I had hoped to be morphed into one of the sixties Goddesses. She soon put paid to that dream!

What was clear to me was that I had to get a very good Leaving Certificate as there was no place for girls at home in the country. The boys were destined to be on the farm. Good luck, bad luck who knows. We thought they were the lucky ones. I am sure they at times envied us our freedom to leave.

Attitudes towards women's place in society were beginning to change with the Women's Liberation Movement but not fast enough! John Banville the novelist clarified it for me in a radio interview. His father lived a simple life, going to work, coming home mid-day for dinner, returning to work and going for a pint before coming home in the evening. His mother's first sign that she was in favour of the Women's movement was to wear a pair of slacks, or trousers as they were called then. She encouraged her children in every way possible but she herself was angry in later years as she felt duped by Church and Society. My own mother would have felt the same way. She was extraordinarily talented but she felt cheated by life.

That year was dreadful for the farming community as cattle prices hit an all-time low and my father was under huge financial pressure. He did what he knew best and buried his head in the sand and hoped it would all go away. He was bordering on a total breakdown. "Go and see if you can do something with your father," was frequently requested. As if I could be of any help! She was on her own, with a very young family and no support. Mental health issues were terrifying for people as there was little understanding. The pressure of that year took its toll and though I did my very best to study I was a nervous wreck at the end of it. I went back to Dublin for the summer to John and Pat and the carefree teenager of the previous year turned up at their door a broken human being. I experienced my first panic attacks shortly after I returned to Dublin. I had no idea what was happening to me and felt that I was going off my head. I wanted to curl up in a ball in my room and stay there. Having to face the outside world was frightening. My need for love and approval was so chronic that I buckled under the smallest demands. It is clear now that I needed rest and counselling. I needed parental support. They couldn't give what they hadn't got. My parents couldn't help themselves, never mind me. I was running on empty. The local doctor in Dublin prescribed Valium and told me to pull myself together. There were no experts for panic attacks. No one seemed to know what they were about. No thought brought them on, they crept up on me and afterwards the fear of them ever happening again terrified me.

My Aunty Bea suffered a nervous breakdown in her mid-forties. One friend asked her to go on holiday and build herself up and another recommended a psychiatrist. She told me the mistake she made was to go to the psychiatrist because she became dependent on medication for the next fifty years. I kept that in mind. I had to be brave and move through each day not understanding what lay beneath my distress. I never spoke of the panic attacks for years as if it was something to be ashamed of.

My father was clear. There was no way he would waste good money on a girl's education only to find she would get married. He had a point then, as girls had to retire on marriage. That was 1969.

Girls earned less than their male counterparts as it was the law. Only when we joined the European Union in 1973 were married women allowed keep their jobs.

I was now cowed by my experience. I felt that if I worked hard I would get the validation and assurance I needed. I was afraid to say to John and Pat that I was experiencing the panic attacks in case they thought I would be too much of a nuisance so I went full steam ahead in trying to do my best. They were helping me investigate some training programmes and we settled for a secretarial course in Dún Laoghaire. I was happy with this because it meant that I could stay with them and I appreciated that security. I had no problem with study but felt isolated in the group. All the girls knew each other from their schools and I was a newcomer. I didn't make friends because I was too vulnerable and emotionally distressed.

The college brought back the fears and the isolation of the transition between local school and convent school. I had neither the confidence nor the social skills to deal with this new environment! By November I was experiencing acute pain in my left side. The doctor sent me to hospital for tests and I was discharged with the diagnosis that it was psychosomatic. Those pains eventually emerged four years later as a huge twisted ovarian cyst. It baffled doctors as to how it had gotten to that stage. I told them that I was told it was psychosomatic and I had dismissed the pain as being imaginary. That is how naive I was! I didn't want to rock the boat, cause trouble. Good girls do not do that.

I went to my local doctor who knew me from birth and spilled out my story of isolation and loneliness. What I was really looking for was a sympathetic detached listening ear and an encouraging word to say I could actually do this course. By the time I had finished talking to him I was ready to return to Secretarial College. He too gave me medication for depression. It helped with the panic attacks. I asked him not to inform my parents.

Instead he advised them that I quit College. Quitting College meant they did not know what to do with me. My mother said, "You are going to have to go back to Dublin because there is nothing for you here." This was casually announced as she was making pastry for an apple tart. She was not saying anything that I did not already know. In challenging circumstances like this she too buried her head and it was up to me to find a solution.

In this way she was following her own mother's pattern of response. This was familiar to her. I was lucky in her mind; at least I had a place in Dublin. She at the same age had been married. We all revert unconsciously to what we know, to what we remember, when we are stressed. It is like placing a finger on a raw nerve. That nerve can live happily until it is pressed by a situation. My father drove me back to Dublin. He was very happy and deposited me at John and Pat's door. He handed me ten shillings. "All the best," he said and drove off. I had the bus fare for a week to find a job.

What doesn't kill you makes you stronger and I went into Dublin the next day to a recruitment agency? I took the first job I was given in the office of Alfred Bird & Sons in Ship St. I didn't think I had other options. Though my parents were not prepared to help me they were not impressed that I found a job in the office of a jelly factory. I worked in the Order Department at first. I had to get used to taking and receiving orders from shops around the country and dealing with Sales Representatives. They sent me on a course to learn how to touch type. It was to prove invaluable later.

I was in Bird's for a year when the Banks in Ireland went on strike. To get into the Bank prior to this I would have needed to complete the secretarial course that I had quit in Dún Laoghaire. You also needed influence or a sponsor as they called it then. I didn't have either. There was such a back log of work after the strike that they had to change their rules of entry. I applied and got in.

We were sent to do an introductory course in Hume House in Dublin. We were given awful brown uniforms but I saw it as a status symbol. I had joined the ranks of the privileged in society. I was doing my best to learn the ropes but it wasn't good enough for the tutor. I see me quietly sobbing as she lambastes me for making an error. It was a totally different atmosphere to Alfred Bird & Sons. Nobody spoke harshly to me there. If I made a mistake I was shown the correct way. In Hume House I was plummeted back in my mind to Primary School. This old wound emerged. It didn't take much to bring it to the surface. We carry our wounds wherever we go. There is no escape until we deal with them.

At the end of the week we were given our posts. I was to go to the Bank of Ireland in Arva, Co. Cavan. I was the only person in the group to be sent to the country. I went home to Pat and John who were very proud that I had succeeded in getting this position and told them I was leaving. They kindly asked if they could see if it was possible to change it for me but I had a feeling that it was time for me to move on. I was and am still very grateful to both of them for everything they did for me. I had some notion that I was going to have a fresh start. My slate was clean. Now I would be confident and positive. What I did not understand then but do now is that we carry our baggage wherever we go. I could not see then why nasty things happen to good people, why good people can become doormats for family and friends. I was a long way from seeing that only when "good" people are pushed to their limit will they find their voice. I have come to look at obstacles differently.

We carry our wounds wherever we go. Change of scenery does not alter that fact. Only when you cultivate self-awareness through self-reflection are you able to see exactly where and why you create your anger. Your anger is a sign that you are trying and failing to control other people and events.

The excitement of having what was considered a great pensionable job and one that would give me a gratuity on marriage was wonderful

CHAPTER 6

Living My Script

'When you know better, you do better'
Maya Angelou

THE first twenty years established patterns of behaviour, habits, fears and beliefs about life and me that I accepted without questioning. The next twenty was living out the impact of that experience.

Moving to Arva was the beginning of the second phase. The excitement of having what was considered a great pensionable job and one that would give me a gratuity on marriage was wonderful. What would people say, what would people think of me now that I was important?

My father was delighted. In fact, he informed me that it was because of his influence I got the job! I let my father think his thoughts, as it wasn't worth an argument. In his own way he was proud but could not say it either. He was like a man on a mission until we got to Arva. When we finally arrived he looked a bit deflated. The image in the head did not match the reality. I felt the same. This was a one street town with an old fashioned draper shop, a couple of sweet shops, a Volkswagen garage, about ten pubs cum shops and what looked like a hotel of sorts. I was soon to find out that a bus went in and out of Arva on a Thursday.

As first impressions were not great we headed to the local hotel to see if I could get accommodation. I was told I could stay for three days as the lads from the local banks lived there. There was no such thing as an apartment in the town. Female bank officials had to stay in digs. I rented a bedroom in the house of Mrs Cowen, a kindly elderly lady. Meals were provided and a close eye kept on my comings and goings. I wasn't going to go very far. I had no car. To test the waters my father decided that we should have what was called high tea. That consisted of two thick slices of roast beef with plenty of fat, two leaves of lettuce and a sliced tomato with brown bread and a pot of tea." You won't do too badly here," he said, "because this is a great feed." I wondered how in God's name I was ever going to get out of the place.

Loel, who was Assistant Manager in my new bank saw my plight. He took me under his wing and taught me much about banking that was to be of great assistance later. Now and again he might have to give me a pep talk, never once did I feel demeaned. It wasn't in his nature. Though I only stayed there for a year and a half, his wisdom and kindness still remain with me. What I will always remember is the echo of his hearty laugh, his phenomenal sense of humour and his acceptance of what is.

There was one main office and a small adjoining room to interview people. That was it. I had to learn quickly about all aspects of office work and within two weeks I was put in my favourite job as cashier. Prior to this you had to have four years' service in the bank before you could be promoted to cashier. It came with a substantial salary increase. I arrived at a time when this rule was changed. I was allowed do the job without the increment. I did get valuable experience.

My discomfort with saying no played out in many funny circumstances. This young fellow came in to the bank looking for a loan. Knowing his background, Loel said he couldn't sanction it. I, seeing his disappointment, encouraged Loel to look again and see if it were possible. I told him that he couldn't tar all family members with the same brush. I hated to see him go cap in hand. Loel relented. My advice did not come from looking at the reality of the situation but a discomfort with hurt feelings. I was working from my memories of humiliation when I had to ask for money. I asked Loel later if he ever recovered the loan. "Not at all," he replied. We laughed.

Arva changed the direction of my life. Within a week I was to meet my future husband who worked in another local bank. He was away on holidays when I arrived and I met him at what was locally known as the Bride's Drink. A local couple had gotten married and a big marquee was set up for a supper and dance. Loel could not go for whatever reason and when he inquired about the night he was told by the manager with a grin on his face from ear to ear that it was a tall tale. This reference was to the fact that my intended husband was almost two metres tall.

I was only twenty years old and though I loved living with my family in Dublin I had no social life. A country girl in Dublin with no school friends or associates doesn't get the chance to meet others and here I was in a small town with someone from another bank who was taking an interest in me. I was completely blown away by it. My own over the top neediness to be loved kicked in big time. He was good company - witty, kind and he had this fantastic new car so we travelled the countryside after work. I felt so at ease with John. In the first flush of the relationship I saw perfection. I had little experience in close relationship skills. I was of the belief that as he was so kind and caring nothing would ever change that. We were like two kids. Heaven lasted so long as it was just the two of us.

The dynamics and the strains began when we had to connect with reality and families. He brought me to visit his grandparent's home in Co. Sligo. It was set on a hill overlooking a beautiful valley. There is a sacredness about the land that is indescribable. We went down to the local quarry to meet the next door neighbour, Eddie Doherty. His bright eyes and broad grin reminded me of my own grandfather. He brought me up to visit his wife Annie Teresa. We sat in their kitchen with its burning range cooker and pictures of the Sacred Heart and had tea and Swiss roll. I was anchored.

Trouble began in our heavenly relationship when I telephoned John at his home. He had been transferred to Dublin and was back living with his parents. I asked to speak to him and when asked who was calling I did not leave my name. I was innocent in these matters. I was greeted crisply. Mother had heard we had visited

Sligo and she wasn't pleased. The icy tone left me under no illusions. There was never going to be a good time to meet her. We landed in on a family occasion. It was the anniversary of his uncle's death and a meal was organised for his aunt. The occasion would be a buffer zone, John mentioned in passing. I did not know what he meant. When questioned if I smoked I knew I had passed some test. Both my parents were chain smokers at that time and I think I had inhaled enough smoke to last me a lifetime. "Was I a picky eater?" was the next question. My reply was that I came from a large family and if you were to survive you had best get over pickiness. I could see the smile on his father's face. He knew what was happening. Did I go to Mass? I did. The tension eased. I was a child who had passed an important test. If a wise person was looking at this situation I would have been asked "Why do you fear so much?" Why did John need a passive-aggressive approach to introduce an important relationship? Later I understood. Why did I think that if I lost this relationship I would never find another one?

John's mother had plans for her family. It is in this area that the real trouble thrived. She had expectations and demands and we were meant to live up to them. She had worked all her life to create wealth and prosperity and had a dream that her family continue where she left off. She was multi-talented and multifaceted. She had authority beyond measure and could face down the most powerful of individuals. I was no match for her. She certainly did see me as being good for her son because if she didn't she would have seen to it that this relationship ended.

After nine months we told them we were getting engaged and she was very happy. She decided she knew best when it came to looking for a ring. I thought that this really was none of her business and tentatively said this but we were too young in her mind to get a good deal. She went around different jewellers looking for discounts and told them the trays to produce when we arrived. My simple wish was to look in The Happy Ring House on

O'Connell Street. This was a famous landmark. When she saw the ring we had chosen she demanded to know its price. I didn't feel she needed to know and stayed quiet. How was I to know that very few people succeeded in challenging her? The same tune was being played out again and again in my life. I, nor John were equipped to challenge her.

When John was transferred to Dublin, Loel used to bring me to Dublin on Friday's. John was to meet me and we were to go out for a meal to celebrate our anniversary of meeting. Just as we were getting into town, Loel noticed John's car driving in the opposite direction with his mother in the front seat. I thought there must be some mistake, so we followed them and discovered they were on their way to visit an old friend of hers. I couldn't understand this because we had made a booking and nothing had been communicated to alter it. I joined them and waited outside this lady's house for a long time as she conducted whatever business she had with her. When she returned she said, "It is too late now for you to go out!" I got the impression that this visit to her friend was a deliberate ploy. I felt the occasion was important to me and quietly insisted we go out as planned. That was until we were in the restaurant. I felt an unease. I took courage and questioned John but he dismissed it. I can remember that feeling of uncertainty; something had changed since he was transferred to Dublin. I did not trust that feeling. People got married very young then. I could have gone back to Arva and stayed in digs but the dream of my own home would have gone out the window. I thought if we were in our own home then nothing could come between us.

Plans began for the wedding. I feared this. The expectation was that we would have a large wedding. I knew my father would not want to fork out money for a large wedding. It was always going to be a problem. Despite all the good intentions, weddings in our house were always traumatic affairs. There was no question of any one of them going smoothly. My mother took on an alter ego when it came to weddings. A fault had to be found somewhere. At my sister's wedding my father's remark was classic. He couldn't cope with the idea that she was marrying a Protestant. When nothing could be done about it he declared, "Well, at least no one will know by the colour of him that she is marrying one of them." I thought that I would escape such troubles because in my case I had all the ingredients for a good marriage. He came from a good family. He was Catholic and had a pensionable job. What more could you want?

My siblings were much younger and couldn't be of help even if they wanted to be. I booked my favourite local hotel. The Park Hotel was always preferred by family and by chance I discovered that my mother had booked a totally different hotel owned by relatives that she barely knew. She didn't tell me about it and wouldn't discuss it when I found out. I was caught between two very powerful women and made the mistake of challenging my mother thinking that she would be the easiest to persuade. I did not feel she was a match for my future mother-in-law. An illusion! Having a wedding in my mother's choice of hotel would have ignited mother–in–law's wrath and this was why I decided to say to my mother that there was no way I could change the venue because my mother–in–law would have a fit. That was when the war began. This was the first time I had ever questioned my mother and it was devastating. I believed she would support me. I felt that she would be the one to save the day. She was beautiful looking and when she dressed up she could be taken for a film star. She had an amazing sense of style. My mother was used to me giving in. Never before had I taken such a stance. Every manipulation was used to no avail. I understand now that there was nothing personal in this high drama. Weddings brought this piece up in her. It never changed. I wanted this whole thing over and done with so that we could begin our lives on our own. After many failed attempts at compromise, it was decided I get married at the Airport Church in Dublin - not my local church. I really wanted that so much.

I had to resign from my position in the Bank on marrying and as I wrote my letter of resignation I felt very anxious. I hadn't fully thought it through. I was following the norm at the time. I loved working in the bank. I sacrificed that life because I needed love, security and a sense of belonging. Though my actual age was twenty-one, my emotional age was probably half that. The mask I created was one that appeared strong and capable.

The week before leaving Arva, my colleague Kathleen and I decided to do a bit of shopping in Cavan. Barney from the local bakery told us that if we went in on the bus he would collect us later. Neither of us had a car. All we had to do was wait under the clock in Cavan town at 6 pm. As we waited there we saw the bus move off. No sign of our transport. In the end we had to hitch hike home. We managed to get back some of the way on a tractor, then on a van full of cables and the last part of the journey was on foot. I couldn't remember when I laughed so much.

When I arrived in Arva I was a colourful little being. I discovered while working in Dublin what clothes suited me and I loved style. I went to the poshest store, Brown Thomas, in Dublin when I got my first pay cheque. I had a facial and bought a beautiful lilac dress with matching suede sandals. Hot pants were in fashion and I purchased an all in one black hot pants suit with white knee high boots. It was some statement. That was the Liz, John fell in love with. I was young and free. Since getting engaged all monies had to be saved! Family influences dominated. Nothing could be wasted as all was to go toward some future plan. No entertainment was considered. The joy had gone! The fear was being on one income. I had not considered the full impact of this and what dependency would really do to me. Panic attacks returned! I had begun to taste independence when I received my first salary and now I was heading back to being dependent. I could feel the change happening in me but could neither communicate nor comprehend what I was feeling.

I left Arva a month before the wedding. There was so much tension at home that I could not go there. I went up to stay with

John's family and promptly developed flu. I was really sick. His father was the gentlest of souls. He nursed me like a small child. He used to make a concoction called egg nog. It was beaten egg, sugar and brandy and it tasted delicious. He came and sat with me and told me stories that made me laugh. We sat by the fire in the sitting room that March of 1973 and he played his favourite music - Joseph Locke, Paul Robeson and Maria Callas. When I was better we walked along the sea front to Portmarnock. He was a wonderful story teller and captivated me with stories of his involvement in Ireland's fight for freedom. Later, I wished I had asked him more about that time. I felt comforted in having a father figure who loved, supported and was a voice for me in difficult times.

We had applied for a mortgage for a house on Griffith Ave. It was beautifully situated on a tree lined avenue, with its bay fronted window. As a bank official at that time you were entitled to a mortgage at 3% where the rest of the people had to pay upwards of 12%. This was an incredible benefit and why the Bank was one of the most sought after jobs. The Manager of the Bank refused to authorise the mortgage for whatever reason.

You did not say no to John's mother. She had admired that house for years. There was an extension at the back which would have made it possible for us to live downstairs and to rent out the top. We wouldn't have been entitled to the 3% but the rental would have paid for the mortgage. She bought the house and managed to secure a loan for us.

One Friday I came up to find the house had been sold. Not a mention of it to me. There was no discussion as to why. When I got upset about it, it was seen as my being over reactive. At this stage my job was gone, my mother wasn't speaking to me and it was only a few weeks until the wedding.

The search began for a new house. Mother-in-law was in her element. House hunting was her passion. We found a lovely house in Woodpark in Ballinteer in immaculate condition. The wedding was only a month away. This mortgage was approved. Though it was difficult for me to admit it, this house was better for us. An added bonus was the fact that it didn't have a phone. There was a waiting list then of about two years. Mother-in-law could only contact us during working hours!

We moved our small belongings in on St. Patrick's Day, a week before the big day. We hired a van that carried all of our goods and chattels. I loved putting everything in its place. On the way back we went to Mass in Adam and Eve's church so we were late getting back home. She froze us out of it. Why hadn't we let her know? There were no phones near and mobile phones hadn't yet been invented. That silence continued until his father stepped in and said, "Leave the child alone." As long as he was there, I had a buffer. I wanted peace with my family and I went home for a few days. Immediately I was met with my mother's anger. It was too much and I fainted. I was recovering from flu and wasn't well. Before I left I said goodbye to my father. It was the first real communication I ever had with him. "I didn't want this," he said. "I know," I replied. He wasn't able to stop it either. I learned how to be silent in a good school.

I returned to Dublin. I had to collect my dress from the dressmakers. Our car had broken down and I had to take a bus. It took an hour to get into town and another hour to get to Skerries. I arrived at that lady's door and when she saw the state of me she invited me in for something to eat. I had lost so much weight and hadn't fully recovered from the flu. I was also very depressed but hid it in an appearance of calm. There was no one I could talk to and there was no one clear sighted enough to say, "You are only 21 years of age, why not call it all off until you are mature enough?" I don't know any of my friends who thought like that. We were in Cinderella land! When I eventually made my way up the steps to the little road that led to the house I was exhausted. The welcome I received from both of John's parents was warm, and I was immediately put at ease with hot food and steaming coffee. I was disarmed by her kind welcome. Perhaps she is always going to be like this now. I could recover in the glow of the love and warmth of that room. A roaring fire was lit in the sitting room and I took out the dress and hung it up. They both looked at each other nostalgically and she asked her favourite question. "How much did the dress cost you?" "Fourteen pounds," I said. She took a deep breath and looked at him in disbelief. He smiled lovingly at me and nodded his head. She shed a small tear and said, "I am just being foolish," and left. We sat quietly and listened to music.

This was the extraordinary dichotomy of mother-in-law. She could be kindness personified and for no apparent reason she could go into an almighty huff that could last weeks. This is what caused confusion in the relationship. I never understood what pressed her buttons but when they were, some old hurt came to the surface and she inflicted it on anyone who was around to receive it. What I didn't have, was the clarity or confidence or emotional intelligence to hand it nicely back to her and say, "This does not belong to me." I was trying to please everyone and could never succeed. I certainly was not able to feel good about myself because I was too overwhelmed and a slave to other people's emotions as well as my own. I could not see the collateral damage.

The idea that this wedding day was mine got lost in everyone else's demands and expectations. Trying to please everyone is a trap. I wanted a quiet peaceful life. Being a rescuer I felt I could do this with pleasantness. Being pleasant to difficult people and acquiescing to their demands creates the perfect environment for becoming a doormat. More to the point, why did I not see that this was not going to change? If I had been able to see that, then it might never have reached the crescendo it did. I kept repeating the same old patterns. I could never find peace until I was at peace with myself. I could not find that peace because I thought the people in my life were disturbing it not the programme that was running wild in my subconscious mind. The person who threatened that peace was giving me an opportunity to stand up. You can't learn anything about yourself when you do not see that you have something to learn. You can't change until you see that you are reacting from your memories. We keep going around in circles until we see this.

I was never one for having to have a big material show, but I knew the wedding dress pattern that I had found in a Vogue pattern book was me. My greatest expense was on a haircut with a hairdresser that only women of my vintage would remember - Robert in The Witches Hut. We would actually sit on the floor and wait patiently for these Celestial Beings to cut our hair. We were exiting the era of the perm and back combing and entering the world of cutting technique. He cut my little sister's hair. She looked so cute. She was seven years old. I sat with my friends Kate and Margaret the night before the wedding in a room above their bakery on Cabra Road. Kate, a school friend was my bridesmaid along with my two sisters. On the morning of the big day John's brother came to see if I needed help. I just needed someone to collect my bouquet of simple fuchsia. My father arrived in great spirits that morning. I imagine he had a few whiskeys to fortify himself to help him cope with the day. He was so engrossed in recounting stories to the driver that he didn't notice the ash from his cigarette fall on my dress. I blew it off. Our local family doctor was waiting outside the church and he said "Liz, all your problems are over now."

The ceremony is just a blur. I remember looking at the altar and realising I never thought of flowers. Then quietly smiling because there had been a wedding before ours and the flowers were beautiful. On the night of the wedding we went for a meal on our own up to Lamb Doyle's, a really nice restaurant half way up the Dublin Mountains and overlooking the city. I felt that this was what I had been looking for. It was going to be just the two of us from now on, living in our own home, making our own decisions for our lives. I felt that I was right to keep on going that once I could be with John on my own all would be well. What I was longing for was that initial Nirvana. Reality was not the problem, my inability to deal with reality was.

I see you through my filter, you see me through your's. Reality is not the problem our perception of reality it.

CHAPTER 7

The Honeymoon is Over

'Do you know why your soul-mirror does not reflect as clearly as it might? Because rust has begun to cover it. It needs to be cleaned'

Rumi

I UNDERSTAND myself enough now to know that I need time and space to assimilate the new. It is not stubbornness or unwillingness to change but processing time, understanding my personal rhythm! I do not like being bombarded or railroaded into something that I have not had the time to mull over. Being comfortable with the known, I need a clear mind before I proceed into the unknown.

I was very nervous about the prospect of flying to go on honeymoon. This had more to do with the amount of stress I experienced prior to the wedding. My body needed rest. Times were very different in Ireland then; travelling was not the everyday experience of ordinary folk. What I actually needed was a holiday in the sun. What John wanted was a skiing holiday. He loved travel. We flew to Munich and got a coach to St. Anton. I had never skied before and the state of my mind was not too open for risk taking.

The first challenge was the ski slopes at 7am the following morning. We were given little instruction. Many had done this before, so it was all happy clappy. I was pushed onto the T-bars and was pulled up to the top of the hill. At the top, this fellow was waiting to make sure I got off this blessed thing and he pushed me so that I had little option but to keep going at high speed. Each day he muttered something in German to me. It didn't sound too encouraging. I gave him a look that would paralyse him but to my horror on the fourth day in perfect English, he told me I was getting the hang of it! Just when I was beginning to feel comfortable our teacher brought us further up the mountain. We were asked to ski down the side of this mountain over bumps that I could not handle. It was too advanced for me as a beginner and certainly too dangerous. I got so distraught I was pushed to shout, "I came here for a holiday, not to kill myself."

The following day I dug my heels in and refused to go back up. It was too much for me so we went on a day trip to Innsbruck instead. As John had no problem and loved skiing, it appeared as if I was being a drama queen. Strolling around Innsbruck I felt very lightheaded. I thought perhaps if I drank a cup of coffee or ate an apple from one of the vendors it might ease. It didn't. I knew I was in trouble of some sort and wanted to get back to St. Anton. We got to the train station and I collapsed. We hadn't the language and there was no one to help, so John lay me down on a bench while he ran for a taxi to take me to the hospital. I could feel myself slipping deeper and deeper into unconsciousness when he returned. He carried me into the car and the driver raced to the hospital. My blood pressure was very low. John was honest when he said he was worried that he had taken on too much responsibility and wondered if he could handle it. The person he had first met was strong and full of life and energy. The person he married was a physical and emotional wreck.

I had no job to go back to. I felt dependent and uncomfortable asking for something because I knew we were going back to one salary. I hated dependency. My conditioning from home kicked in. I wouldn't demean myself by asking. I plummeted right down into the depths of my own conditioning. I couldn't wait to get home. The closeness I felt the night we married seemed a long way away. I was not aware of my unconscious expectations of him to be my happiness. I knew if I was to survive I had to find a way out of this dependent mess.

On the way back into Dublin the plane hit an almighty air pocket. Darkness descended as it plummeted down. It seemed to drop out of the sky but it righted itself and there was an audible sigh of relief. It found its balance. Perhaps this was what was happening to us. We had hit reality. I felt that no matter what problems we had we could sort them out now that we were back on familiar ground. We were very young and I knew nothing about love other than what was in Mills and Boon stories in Women's Weekly. I was ill prepared for married life. No birth is easy and birthing yourself from illusion is extremely painful. "Love is blind, marriage is an eye opener," my next door neighbour told me the week before we married. Love is never blind, romantic conditioning is blind but never love!

The ideas I had on what love actually was, were based on ideas of a knight in shining armour rescuing me from my life. I had very little experience in relationships to see that the only rescuing knight would eventually be myself.

If he needed me to be strong that was also my expectation of him. If he wanted security I, too, wanted the same except foolishly we wanted the other to provide it for us.

Happiness starts with you.

It is a known fact that the family member we have greatest difficulty with is the one we can turn out to be like if we are not conscious of the morphing over the years

CHAPTER 8

After the Ecstasy the Laundry

'Love is never blind; infatuation is blind'

Anthony de Mello

TWO suitcases full of dirty laundry earths you quickly enough when you return. We had to go out to shop for a washing machine. John was of the belief that a twin tub washing machine was not only a better quality machine but also much more economical. I grew up in the age of the bulky washing machine. One that was pulled in front of a sink with a roller for pulling sheets through it! A big farmhouse was capable of hiding such a monstrosity. The latest version of this was a bit neater but still worked on the same principles. I loved our new home. It was reasonably spacious yet compact. The previous owners had a sense of style and used space wisely. The kitchen, though small had a place for everything necessary - including an automatic washing machine. To me the machine we bought was an eyesore.

It is a known fact that the family member we have greatest difficulty with is the one we can turn out to be like if we are not conscious of the morphing over the years. The transition is obvious to anyone but the person experiencing the morphing. Stress brings the similarities to the surface. Challenge can push us into our default mode and if we are not aware of it we revert back to our known ways of response. Mother-in-law had a ferocious appetite for a bargain. Haggling was a game. Though John would say he was mortified every time she did this, once he was faced with living without the support of home and spending his money, the need for a bargain emerged and he was adept at achieving this aim. As soon as I heard the request for a discount, I would descend into an abyss. I may as well have been standing in front of my father asking for money. I had no stomach for it. It brought me back to the feeling of going cap in hand for small returns. The cellular memories of feeling shamed!

The sudden responsibility of married life seemed to push him into his comfort zone of what was familiar to him. I descended into mine which took the form of agreeing even though every part of my being wanted to say' No', but he had the cheque book. A feeling of helplessness took root. Don't rock the blessed boat. Be grateful you are getting a washing machine. We both retreated to the familiar. Even though the familiar was painful, it was a pain we both knew well. This made it acceptable. I gave the impression that I agreed. When I did give an opinion strongly he appeared to agree with me at first. Over time he planted a seed of doubt, then another and another until such time as we were back to square one. Nothing gained! His father told me once, that this was how he handled his wife. He smiled disarmingly when he announced that. I could really understand why he did this.

Then a miracle happened. The marriage ban ended and I reapplied for a position in the bank. The banks took back skilled married staff on a temporary basis but at a lower salary. I went for interview and I was immediately employed. My first position was in the Montrose bank situated opposite University College Dublin. Montrose meant that I could go and visit my sister who had just begun her first year at University. Even my father was moving with the times. The College was situated directly across the road from the bank and I met her for lunch. The daily visit meant that it took the mystery out of the College experience.

While in Montrose some Inspectors arrived from Head Office. Seeing my work, they recommended that I do the Bank exams because they were looking at the prospect of promoting me. My first response was fear. If I did get a promotion it might undermine our relationship. I didn't have leadership skills because I couldn't handle authority. This thinking was not the case in John's household where his mother was a dominant character. I had no awareness that my reaction was a pattern, or that there could be a different way. Those beliefs constituted my reality. To question them would have destabilised me. John would have had no problem with my promotion; in fact, he was completely encouraging in the years that followed. He would have loved nothing better than my accepting positions that would have improved our financial position. This was familiar to him. Mother was very strong so being in the shadow of a strong female was normal to him. Shortly afterwards I was made permanent. Being back at work and doing something worthwhile gave me a sense of self-worth and freedom. Every penny I earned I saved for that rainy day. There was no time for fun. We rarely ever went out other than to visit friends and I felt guilty spending on myself. This diligence brought the approval I needed. I didn't grow up in a family with goals. We muddled through!

In the meantime, mother-in-law was relentless in her wish that I go and do further study. This is what she had done. She said that having a qualification for her meant that no matter what happened she had a pensionable job. Her job gave security to the family when father-in-law was ill for many years. You couldn't argue with that logic. I too felt that I had missed out on a College education. My obstacle was my feelings of self worth.

There was a strike at University College Dublin in 1974 and though it was October, registration had not taken place. One day I decided to go to the admissions office and see what was on offer. Mother-in-law had offered to pay half the course fees should I choose Primary Teaching. I was undecided because any course would involve giving up my permanent job.

Something propelled me to enrol in University College Dublin and I chose to do History, Geography and Economics. I ran down the steps and felt elated with the decision. I telephoned my mother-in-law to say I had registered. She wasn't happy with my choice saying she wanted me to study Irish if I were to continue with this choice. Though I was clear on why I wanted these subjects she hadn't given up on her demand. To me they were practical and in English. She came to visit me. Without losing any time she proceeded to place her chair right in front of me, folded her arms and spoke in a menacing clipped tone to emphasise her point of view. I was not a lemming and there was no way I was studying Irish. I hadn't spoken it for five years. I was grateful we did not have a house phone over the ensuing weeks. I stayed well clear of her. She had resistance to financially supporting this enterprise because I was not doing what I was told. Lectures began in early November of 1974. History was fascinating especially Irish History. It was a whole new world. I loved going back to father-in-law and telling him about what was happening. I can't ever remember being so happy before. I wanted to share all I was learning about a time he had lived through. University gave me an energy and an interest beyond my wildest dreams. I blossomed those first weeks.

Then it happened. That day we all hope might never happen. That reality we do not wish to face. We had given our neighbour's telephone number in the event of an emergency and we got a call to say father-in-law had a slight turn. We immediately went to the hospital and were assured that everything was under control and he was fine. We were allowed in to see him. He was wired up to machines. He put out his hand to me and said that he had only two fingers free and could only give me the John Murray handshake. John Murray never proffered anything more than two fingers. Though he was anxious, he was in good form. We went home with mother-in-law and sat there drinking tea, each of us in our own thoughts. As the night passed we felt reassured and went to bed. The shrillness of the phone broke the silence. He had another heart attack. We were there in minutes. The doctor said, "He knows you are here." I wanted to sit with him. I didn't want him to feel alone. He died early that morning.

It was wet, windy and cold the day of the funeral. Eddie Doherty came as did others from his youth. He was loved by many because he touched their hearts. Anthony de Mello says we grieve not for the person gone but for ourselves, our loss. That surely is true because the first thought that came to me was what would I do without his love and protection, his sense of humour and the security of having him as a buffer between me and mother-in-law? She had the capacity to take over your life and demand you live it on her terms. I was broken hearted when he died. There was no escape from her demands. Not even holidays were sacred as you would get a letter telling you what needed to be done when you came back. The previous year they left for Galway and she left her usual instructions on a piece of paper. Water the tomatoes, cut the grass, and trim the hedges, on a piece of cardboard. My father-in-law, on the other hand, wrote on the back of it – and if you have any energy left, sweep the streets from here to Portmarnock with a toothbrush and so many other things that made me laugh till I cried. I looked at the card and said, "This must be kept. One day he will be gone and how do you describe his quirky sense of humour more accurately than this?"

He loved when we visited him in Sligo. He could have happily lived out the rest of his years there. On one of our visits we were informed that we must bring down our best Sunday suits for Mass. That was the custom and you had to be attired in the very best. We obeyed. All went well with the local Canon who was saying Mass until it came to his Sermon. He seemed to have the force with him as he strode towards the pulpit. He settled himself and placed his two huge hands on the front of the pulpit and looked venomously at his silent and expectant congregation and roared "If I catch any of yisser childer in my apple trees I'll batter them." At this stage he was so livid with rage he was almost dancing on the altar. I got such a shock when he started that I began to rock with laughter. I did my best to keep it in. The tears were streaming down my face. I took one look at father-in-law and saw him mopping tears as well. Mother-in-law looked at us. "You," she said to me, "are bad but he is worse. I will deal with you both later." She meant it. He looked at me with that twinkle in his eyes. "I think you and me are in the dog house." How can you replace someone like him? So it is correct. We grieve for our loss not his. We act out of self-interest if we are truly honest.

I continued to study but found it a strain. I did not have good study skills. The exhilaration of attending lectures dissipated when faced with the reality of passing exams. Fear of exams crippled me. Setting a goal and targets was difficult for me. Prioritising and time management were not my strong points. That would have meant me having the ability to stand up for what was important for me. I did not have that freedom. The nice person image is a difficult one to live with. There was no one I could go to for help. Being older than the majority of the students, it was expected that I should know how to deal with this. Nothing like pending exams to focus the mind! The fear that I would be a failure kicked in fast and furiously. Many people felt it their moral duty to inform me that I was crazy for giving up a good job because what guarantee did I have of passing the exams. I crammed knowledge into my head in the final six weeks. I was a nervous and emotional wreck. I did well in the first papers. I dreaded the Geography exams as the failure rate was very high. When I got through the papers successfully I got so excited. Once I had faced my greatest fear which was Geography that initial high plummeted me to an immediate low. I had one day to revise History. I could not recognise or remember a word of the notes I had so carefully drafted. The words and or but seemed like Greek. I panicked. I had come so far to stumble on the last hurdle. I didn't want to sit the exam but John insisted. He went to our local doctor, got two sedatives and made me take one and brought me to the exam hall and pushed me through the door. Who was I to think I could do this? Who did I think I was? Conditioning is mighty!

July the results were out. They were posted on a window outside the Arts block and all the students clamoured to see if their name had made the cut. Mine was there. I was like Julie Walters in the film Educating Rita. Disbelief, joy and a profound sense of relief all mashed into one. If I could get through the first year, then I could make it all the way. Pushing through my own mental barrier was my Everest. The mind controls you completely if you allow it.

What is extraordinary about education is that I had spent umpteen years at school and had succeeded in cramming knowledge into my brain but basic human interaction was a minefield for me. All those years of education where the focus was on answers and yet questioning was discouraged. This is the way of education and until this is addressed we will continue in the dark. We will remain uneducated! Teachers and leaders with amazing knowledge and limited true relationship skills! You only have to listen to the back biting in any office or staff room to know this is truth. Free people do not need to relate in this negative way. Free people can challenge, without having to diminish the other. Free people are not terrified of giving an opinion and can accept constructive criticism. They create opportunities for self-empowerment. Unhappy people continue to need status, control and power.

Each year had its own hurdles to cross. During my second year in college, I was not feeling well at Christmas, but I put it down to tiredness. I had this niggling pain in my side and hoped it would go away. My psychosomatic pain had come back! I believed that rest would sort it out but didn't have the gumption to state I needed it. Mother-in-law had a car down in Sligo and she wanted it in Dublin for Christmas. She had learned how to drive after she retired and she only ever drove when she was in the country. She was a disaster on wheels. I agreed to go with her on the train and bring the car back up.

Another Christmas without father-in-law's presence and I was in full flight trying to ease the pain. Taking responsibility for another also includes taking responsibility for their emotional pain. You cannot make another person happy but neither can you be responsible for their pain or loss. This is a process each one of us has to go through. Yet the media, literature, songs and our teachers will say that it is our job to make others happy and it is our efforts that generates happiness in them. This is programming!

I knew that Christmas would not be easy for her. I thought of hosting it in our house so that there would be minimum reminders of her loss. All day I was not well. The pain got worse. I didn't want to be a moan but this was too much. I had to give in and go to bed. The pain increased and became unbearable. We had no phone to call a doctor. Mother-in-law came and told me that there were times when I was inclined to be over dramatic and she threw holy water over me. At this stage I was vomiting with pain. As it was Christmas night, no one wanted to call a doctor. I begged John quietly to go and get a doctor. He came back and told me the doctor told him that I should take indigestion tablets that I had probably eaten too much. I had barely eaten. If I had been capable of breaking through my programme of being a martyr, I would have screamed so loud something would have been done. I didn't and nothing happened for hours.

Eventually someone relented and when our own doctor came he got angry. How could they have left me like this? My relief at seeing him brought a floodgate of tears. I was suffering from dehydration. He gave me morphine for the pain to see if it would ease it but it had little effect. He told me to go immediately to hospital and he would telephone ahead to say I was coming. John and I went on our own. I was operated on the following day. It was a twisted ovarian cyst the size of an apple. So much for my psychosomatic pain!

I could sit in judgment on that night and hold on to the resentment and pain of neglect, or let it go. To let it go I had to understand something about myself. How could someone else honour my feelings when I was not in a position of knowing how to honour them myself? How could someone take me seriously when I did not take me seriously? How could someone know what to give me, or how to love me, when I did not know how to love myself? The inability to shout from the rooftops, to demand a doctor from the very beginning, to not care what anyone thought of me was in me. I needed approval, even the approval for being a martyr. Making a fuss was being selfish. What is also interesting is that in my need for security I mistook control for strength. I mistook dominance for guidance. The more I did not speak the more I allowed the other a stronger voice. This way of control is insidious. You do not see it creeping up. I feared reaction, body language, clipped tones, anger, silence and manipulations. Even if I knew I had rights, had a voice, I couldn't do anything about it. I hadn't the courage to follow through. Even if I did speak up, the more I tried to explain myself the more the other was able to convince me that I was a basket case.

That Christmas I had an opportunity to stand up to mother-in-law and missed it. She needed someone to meet her strength of will and it didn't happen. This gave her permission to walk all over me. We all had a part to play in this and it would be many years before I stopped waiting for someone else to put a stop to her gallop for me.

The day I was taken to hospital she went on holidays to Sligo. When she returned she came to visit me. Her first words were whispered in my ear, "Does this mean you can't have any children?" Another person would have been able to say, "None of your business." At what cost to self, did this silence come? For years I judged her. That judgement burned inside me and ate me up. Until one day I saw it for what it was in reality. All of us were operating out of our conditioned minds. At any stage along the way we could let go of that conditioning. We are not our conditioned minds though conditioning is a powerful dictator. Once I saw that, I could step out and be free of that way of thinking. That mind-set trapped me in a spider's web for too long. My ego saw me as the victim. That made me the good person. So long as ego was running the show I would still be hanging on to the old script. The memory is there but there is no pain attached to it anymore. That is freedom!

In my final year I was expecting our first baby Michelle. Nothing prepared me for morning, noon and night sickness or the tiredness. Trying to keep awake while studying was a feat in itself! I was still getting sick when doing the exams. Answering questions on Mussolini and morning sickness was not a great combination but I made it through. Knowing the expected due date was October 17th and the repeats were in August focused my mind. The sense of achievement when I completed the exams was worth the effort. I had every intention of doing the Higher Diploma. This involved getting teaching hours in a Secondary School. I thought it would be easy enough to get a position after Michelle's birth but as she was due in October no school wanted the inconvenience of taking on someone who would need maternity leave as soon as school term began.

I was staff student liaison officer in my third year of College. Professor Dudley Edwards and Dr Michael Richter were on the committee. They seemed to think that I had leadership skills. I didn't know myself. Internally behind the walls of fear they were there, but I hadn't accessed those skills yet. The only reason I took the position was because no one else offered to, and being older I felt responsible.

Michelle's birth changed me. It was like I was complete. Seeing her brought me such joy that I did not want to leave her. Whatever I thought prior to her birth was head stuff, after her birth the heart kicked in. It was easy to be detached and make plans before she was born but nature or nurture, call it what you will, a myriad of unknown feelings changed everything. I was in unfamiliar territory, confused but determined. I knew we could survive financially on one salary. I was adjusting to the needs of a new baby. Mother-in-law did not lose faith in her wish for me to become a Primary School teacher. She discovered that a new course was being offered to graduates where they could do a Primary teaching diploma in one year. To do the course I had to pass an Oral Irish exam. Interviews were set for Easter. It felt right to go ahead and do it. What also made it easier to go ahead with this plan was that I had the support of John and Mother-in-law. She was a woman on a mission. She got me enrolled on an Irish course that was already full and found an Irish speaking family in Spiddal, Galway, who would take me into their home for a month. She was prepared to finance a car for me and we found the sweetest little two tone mini owned by a lady driver. It was immaculate. There was no hesitation and we bought it. We put a roof rack on the top of it, got a car seat for Michelle and I was ready for take-off. Her cot was placed on the rack and she and I headed for Galway. I remember the journey well. I had never driven such a distance before on my own. I was not sure of the way to Connemara. Michelle was oblivious of my anxiety as she sat in her baby seat gurgling and sleeping. We stopped in Athlone to get a bite to eat. I talked to her of my hopes and dreams both for her and for me and she looked at me with those huge eyes as if she understood this young twenty-seven-year-old mother. Michelle has played a huge part in my transformation as a human being. She challenged me to find new ways of parenting. I didn't need to be a clinical psychologist to understand that the parenting I had received would not serve her well.

On this maiden voyage she was only about seven months old and had begun teething. We found the house where we were to stay for a month and reality hit home as to why we were there. The panic attacks returned with a vengeance. I felt isolated and alone. I went to the doctor and he could see I was overwrought. He wondered why I was doing this at this time. What kept me sane was Michelle's smiley face. She was such a happy little baby and between study and walking to the beach we idled our days away. I returned to Dublin, did the interview in Carysfort Teacher Training College immediately before I forgot any of what I had learned, and thankfully got a place. It was a great achievement and I am extremely grateful for mother-in-law's persistence.

The year in College flew by. One of the lecturers told me that I had the potential to be a Principal in five years. I shied away from this prospect in the same way I shied away from promotion in the bank. They seemed to recognise skills in me that I did not see in myself. This is the tragedy of human beings. They see themselves through the filter of their thoughts and beliefs. We all have different filters. Reality and our filters are not the same. My thoughts about myself became my identity. My relationship to self was flawed. I lacked confidence.

My teaching practices went very well and I was given excellent references. It was difficult to get permanent employment but I managed to get a temporary position. I had worked in the Bank while most teachers had gone from school to training. They were more in tune with the system than I. I found it difficult especially in the staff room. I seemed out of place. I needed to look at my attitudes to teachers too, as I had a lot of unhealed memories from my own school experience. 1979 was a different time and place. I resented the power of the clergy as Chairpersons of each school and our lack of freedom as Professionals. Policy and behaviour were dictated not discussed. I felt I was a child again! I loved being with the children but not the system. I wished to be a different kind of teacher as well as being a different kind of parent. What that fully meant I did not know. I could only find out through what it was not. For some time, I swung in the opposite direction to what I had experienced at school and that did not work. My need to be seen as loving got in the way of classroom discipline. I tried to be detached. I understood detachment to mean distance. I believed that I had to change from being a nice person so that I could keep my distance and that meant putting on this cold exterior. That didn't work.

Distance and emotional detachment are totally different principles. Distance is a shutdown of emotions. Detachment allows you freedom. All of your senses are alive and well and you can detach from the behaviour, deal with it calmly and appropriately while being loving at the same time. With detachment you do not need to resort to shouting in order to control. The child will not be diminished by correction. You do not emotionally react. I found myself becoming critical and judgemental of teachers and the system. My old resentments against teachers emerged. Everyone else was out of step. I needed people to change to my image of how they should be for me to become happy. Great! They could all have the privilege of being as messed up as myself! The world's problems could have been solved in an instant if they joined my mental asylum.

I was expecting my second child Grace. She was due the end of August. Michelle wasn't well as her digestive system was in flux. She cried every day I went to work. "Don't go to work today Mum, you stay and play with me." I was torn in two. My dream of the happy family was being challenged! All this study and financial support to ensure I get this far, and here I was looking into the face of a sick child and working in an environment I hated. Teachers had perfect hours when it came to child care. They had long holidays and a pension. They could plan their work from home. Few jobs could give me that freedom. I loved teaching but hated the environment. Was I wasting a great opportunity? I had freedom working in the bank and little or no freedom working in the school. It seemed like a straitjacket.

There had to be a better way for me, a place where I could grow up emotionally. Guilt followed me around like a stalker. I felt the children in the school were not getting enough and my own child was suffering. My organisational skills hadn't improved. I was trying to do too much. I felt inadequate. I wondered if I could organise myself a bit better, if I had less work to do in the home would it be possible to do the two jobs. I knew I needed more help with our second baby on the way and I suggested we get an automatic washing machine. The other one was seven years old by this time. It was time to ditch the old war horse! We bought an automatic washing machine and a dryer. They were not a month in the house when I knew that I was not going back to work.

Sitting down and talking through problems was not part of my vernacular. Even thinking of my father and mother discussing a problem brings a smile. There was no positive template to follow. I ran away from problems, if not physically at least mentally. You bring to problems your own set of beliefs and central to mine was that if I brought what I was thinking out in the open I could be stopped in my tracks. I was aware that I hadn't the capability to stick to my point of view, or to find a compromise that would work for us both.

I knew that if I as much as mentioned what was going on in my head as I was going through the process of thinking it out, I could easily be manipulated. I had to know for sure that this way felt right. There just had to be such an inner knowing like the one I had felt when I went to college. My gut instinct as I understood it, said that I needed to quit at that time. Something about it told me that I could not develop the ideas in my head on what education was all about, if I continued in a system where I felt totally controlled. I couldn't breathe in it. I was no fool either. Mother-in-law would have been brought into this scenario and I was not able to stand my ground. I was not dropping education; I was taking a rest. I was retreating until I understood what way I intended to go. I had no doubt that she would have come out in full force against my plan. She had her problems, my response to her was mine. My silence when she stormed the building was giving her permission to continue in this way. Every step of the way we were challenged to find a bit of back bone. The problem was allowed to escalate. Though she was a problem, she was not the problem.

She needed to move house on a regular basis. Looking at houses was a pastime but buying them an occupation. In the search for another house for her we came upon one that would suit us. Could we raise the money? Fate or Serendipity played a role. I went home and picked up a local newspaper and saw an advertisement where a couple were looking for a house on the road we lived on. Rarely did I ever read this paper let alone read the advertisements. Our house fit their criteria and I picked up the phone and rang the number. I said that it would be ready for viewing in one week as I had visitors at that time. Michelle was three years old and Grace nine months. I painted, wallpapered and scrubbed the house to within an inch of its life. I even borrowed certain pictures and furniture to make it look better. By the time I had finished with it the place looked so good it seemed a pity to move! I knew from the drawings that the other house was detached, and had a huge garden and we would not be overlooked by neighbours. There was no doubt in my mind which house suited us and as we were one of the first to view them, we were in a privileged position to choose the one that suited our needs. It was near shops, schools and a beautiful park. From the sale of our own house we got the exact price we needed. We asked the builders to convert the garage as the house was being built and that is where plan B came into operation. I saw the opportunity to open my own pre-school and develop my own ideas on play and education for life rather than a living.

This didn't go down well with the mother-in-law. As she put it "Not all of us have the luxury of doing what we like. Do you not think it is time to support my son?" "If you don't mind me saying so," was the introduction to all reprimands and not one area of my life did she feel was a no go area. I did not have the gumption to say, "Our life and how we live it is our business not yours. You have had an opportunity to live yours to the full and according to your beliefs. I do not interfere in your life; I do not tell you how you should live it. I do not tell you how you should have reared your children, so please refrain from telling me what I should or shouldn't do as a wife, a mother or person." I never said any of this. She had also supported my education financially so that also silenced me.

This brings me back to Anthony de Mello's statement in his book Awareness. "Please feel free to live your life as you see fit, but allow me live mine as I see fit." We were the problem in our own lives. We allowed ourselves become victims to her and by our example we were teaching our children that this was acceptable behaviour.

What is clear now is that John and I were two emotionally immature people who had little or no skills in dealing with conflict or communication of feelings. I approached difficulties as if I were powerless. We were both controlling in passive aggressive ways, never openly saying what we felt but throwing out the odd comment here and there. This way of communication is not uncommon but it certainly did not serve us. It created the distance we both feared. We say we do not want to hurt the feelings of another but the truth is we are afraid for ourselves. How can you move forward when you do not even know yourself? How can you allow your children to develop when you have no idea you are stuck with old family patterns of behaviour that you will pass on to them? I couldn't answer these questions because I didn't understand their importance. Working with children was my next step in freedom.

The most selfish act is that I demand that you live your life as I see fit according to my beliefs and expectations. Please feel free to live your life as you see fit but allow me to live mine as I see fit.

CHAPTER 9

A Different Kind of Teacher

'On the other side of fear you will always discover freedom'

Robin S. Sharma

W ITH children I have the freedom to be me. They are as they are. They haven't clothed themselves yet in our baggage.

Finn, my grandchild was five years old when he asked me if I loved him and his little brother Oisín more than anything else in the world. I assured him I did. Would I miss him if he were not around? "Yes, I would." "But you would never have known me. How could you miss what you have never known? You really don't know what I am talking about, do you"?

What I love is the directness of children. You know there is no hidden agenda. They state what they see. "Nana, do you see the hair on your chin. Do you cut it with a knife?" This was announced majestically in a packed restaurant and was repeated until the owner of the hairy chin owned up. Directness without malice!

Children are totally present in the moment, there is neither yesterday or tomorrow, there is just now. In their company I do not have to put on any masks. I know I am acceptable to them in my form and they are acceptable to me in theirs. Until you shed unhealthy programmed beliefs about yourself, there will always be thoughts that hold you back from fully experiencing that childlike quality of joy.

Opening my own playschool allowed me creative expression of my talents with children. Once I saw that this could work then there was no going back. Children need freedom to play and explore. They need to progress at their own level and to feel happy and secure in their environment to thrive. Not all children are alike or have the same rate of development. Some love academic work from the beginning, others like a more hands on experience. They learn differently. I wanted the freedom to develop an environment that catered for the needs of individual children. I didn't want to be curtailed by any system.

I have long had serious reservations about the direction of education. Children are asked to accept a rigid curriculum too early in life. Class sizes are too big in those initial years. Whether teachers like it or not they have to train the children to conform. Education now seems to be corporate driven. The emphasis is on academic subjects that feeds the needs of the corporate world. This approach is neglectful of the creative, musical and artistic talents of children. Are our children to become worker bees who must work in occupations that suit big business. If education was about finding the individuality and strengths in our children and guiding them towards that expression, society would be happier. When children enter the school system they must sit for lengthy periods of time. This is unnatural for a small child. Move through the school system and there is an over emphasis on the academic. From the waist down they begin to atrophy. Muscles you do not use you will lose. So, one side of the brain will be more used than the other. How does that make sense? Though the curriculum contains the arts, it is not sufficiently respected. With all of this Education, why is there so much hatred and violence? Why is the Planet being destroyed by greed?

The number of parents in my pre-school who were worried about the implications of a points system that had been introduced by the Department of Education was mind-boggling. From the outset I needed to be truthful. I had to make it clear to them that if this was what they wanted they would be disappointed sending their child to me. I spoke of the value of free play, socializing and the development of skills and ideas, communication, motor development of fine and gross motor skills, fun and friendship as being key players in their child's development. If this need to satisfy a points system was the parent's desire, then they would not be happy with me. Education for life, not just to make a living was my priority. They needed to learn how to relate. I too was learning how to relate through them.

Rosie, one of those children, loved to paint. Mum was always very stylish and so the child's painting portrayed her with colourful earrings, red shoes, bracelets and flamboyant dresses. Once the painting was complete she made a beeline towards the pot of black paint. In Training College, we were told to be vigilant around children who insisted on using black. After a few black Madonna's I asked her outright why she painted her mum black? I got a direct answer. "She goes out at night." So much for my psychology!

The pre-school exuded life. This was just what I wanted, honouring the individuality of every child and giving them an environment to express themselves. Molly was beautiful in every way. She was one of the most balanced children I ever taught. Highly intelligent, she was also musical, loved to play, get stuck in to the messiest games with play dough, water, and paint or cooking. She exuded life. Ted was a very intense little fellow but when it came to Molly his whole face lit up. The moment lunchtime was announced he would rush to take his place beside her. "Why do you choose to only sit beside Molly?" "I love lookin' at her," he replied. An honest man.

I remember reading a book by Alan Watts on how our lives begin to contract after the age of nine. In the beginning the world is our oyster and it is only when outer influences begin to impact on us do we develop beliefs and behaviours to accommodate our environment. I feel this is happening earlier now.

For five years I worked on my own. In the meantime, my third child Paul was born. I needed help. Marie, an old school friend of mine joined me. We both had our strengths. She was brilliant with the little ones and gave me more freedom to work with more challenging children. The challenging children tested the system and helped me in my quest for an alternative approach. When you are vulnerable it is difficult not to personalise behaviours. When a child stands in front of you seething with rage because he or she did not get their way and declares, "I hate you, I hope you die," it is not easy. It triggers you. I found that when I did not react and allowed the child to come through the emotion they felt they were safe. I waited for the anger to pass because it was useless even thinking of communicating at that moment. What was clear was that they had to learn that this behaviour did not work in this environment.

It took time but each and every child who behaved in this way felt secure by the end of the year. It was also important for me to let parents know this was the approach I was taking. When adults are triggered by children and they lose control it is like chaos meeting chaos. When you remain calm there is no fuel for that fire. It has to burn out eventually. It is easier to do this when it is not your own child because most parents react out of fear for their child in the future, or they fear what friends and family think of their parenting skills.

I was always drawn to challenging children. It is funny to see how society applauds the conformists and criticises the child who challenges the norm. It is true they test limits, but it is also true that we need to understand the motive behind the difficult behaviour. What governs our rules? Are they passed down from the previous generation? Are they constructive or do they only serve to have you at loggerheads with your child? This is not about peace and giving in at the least tantrum, it is about really looking at your rules and seeing if they serve any useful purpose.

Children developed my listening skills. They made me discern the difference between a need and a want. The wants are usually the ones that cause the most trouble because the demand gets loud. Wants being met are nice now and again but they are the treats. Some of your beliefs need questioning and they encourage you to go beyond the parameters of your own parents and teachers. You never notice what you see most often. It becomes too familiar. Stopping to look is called discovery. Remember, how your parents and teachers taught you is now obsolete. As the child is born, the world they are born into is not the world their parents were born into. I used to go immediately to my own children when they cried at night or when some minor incident occurred. I discovered this did not give them the skill of self-regulation or independence. They became insecure. My insistence on being there for every little tittle tattle was giving them a message that they could not sort it out for themselves. I was creating anxiety.

Teaching children how to communicate effectively was part of our programme. I wanted them to be comfortable in verbalising their concerns. Some children presented with Attention Deficit Disorder. impulsiveness was a major problem for them. You believe they should have control over their impulses but they don't. By the time the thought reached the head they were like a runaway train. The desire to do whatever was in that head had to be expedited immediately. There was no pause button. The filter did not exist. I paid attention to the triggers and managed somehow to intercept many a disaster. Children with ADHD have a heightened sense of justice. If a child with ADHD perceives that they have been wronged in some way, they over focus on the act and will not be satisfied until justice has been done. I often wonder at it being called ADHD. There is a belief that they never seem to pay attention. The problem is that they pay too much attention to what is being said or done. They take in so much that they are on overload. It is because their minds are congested with details that it is difficult for them to filter out what is required. Processing the detail is their problem. They can focus but it has to be something of great interest to them. It is annoying for teachers to see these children on track in particular subjects that interests them. This could be annoying to a teacher who sees the child not focusing on their own subject. It is heard frequently, "This ADHD is just an excuse for bad behaviour."

Forgetfulness, as they get distracted is a major issue. They are really creative and the unrealised potential is heart-breaking. With the passing years' self-esteem plummets because they think that there is something wrong with them. There is, but not in the way they perceive it. Many film directors, photographers, poets, artists, graphic designers, computer software geniuses have ADHD. John Lonergan, former governor of Mountjoy Prison, said that many of the inmates were undiagnosed ADHD victims. So much potential lost! For a short while it appeared as if the educational system was waking up to the reality that children need to have an emotional connection to their learning to develop their interest and creativity.

I visited a school in Auckland in New Zealand where the children spent equal amounts of time outdoors as well as indoors. When I arrived they were busy constructing items with hammers, nails and wood outside. They were allowed complete the task before returning indoors. As long as they were being constructive and were paying attention to the task they had been asked to do they could remain outside until they felt it was complete. They returned to the classroom to discuss the project and only then did they write about it. This took some time but there was no rush. They had a purpose for reading and writing when it was related to their activities. What the teachers said was that children need breathe in and breathe out activities. If they do something that requires them to listen intently that is a breathe in activity. It must be followed by a breathe out activity. It is too stressful for them to be sitting in chairs and having to listen for long periods of time followed by the intensity of documenting what teacher has just said. They needed time to work things out for themselves as much as possible. It made sense to me. What they also said is that the information stayed with the children when they were involved in their learning. They learned to work in groups, to listen to each other and learn from each other. Though I was not aware of it, this was exactly what we were doing in the playgroup.

When society is advancing at breakneck speed it is difficult to see the gifts in the ordinary happenings of daily life. Ordinary simple play, sharing, cooperating, inventing and having fun is vitally important for a child's natural development. We get caught into the vortex that only the games on offer from large companies are the very best way forward to stimulate children. These toys are like quick fixes. We are looking for the quickest way forward but somehow we are missing an important link. Though these games are colourful and engaging they are not the full answer. Learning to take turns, listen, be creative, accept differences, deal with boredom, being outdoors in the open air are also important aspects. The more we give our children, the more we jump the moment they get bored, the more we sign them up for every activity under the sun the more we deny them the experience of contentment. To look, see and discover is what is important. In the past, children had no childhood because they were treated as young adults. Now their childhood is being robbed because of television, computer games and our expectations. They are being subjected to material that is totally unsuitable and they have no way of processing what they are seeing. What you focus on in your life will grow. The things you invest your intention in grow in importance. We need to be mindful.

During this time, I attended many courses in psychology and counselling to help me move beyond the boundaries of my thinking. I attended a course by Dr. Mark Morgan, Psychologist. I asked a number of questions at the end of the session. He looked at me as if puzzled and said, "It is interesting that all of your questions are related to the defence of children." Feeling a little put down at the time I retreated into my shell. As I reflect now on his remark I see there was truth there. From early childhood I had a strong intuitive need to defend children. It wasn't just children I was defending; I was also defending childhood.

Reading Awareness by Anthony de Mello transformed my teaching. He stated that the unaware life was not worth living. It was easier for me to blame the children's behaviours for my stress levels prior to reading the book. It challenged me to be mindful of what I was bringing to the situation. When I reacted strongly I had to investigate the problem in me and ultimately change my approach. I noticed that with challenging children the strongest desire I had initially was that they just comply. Awareness of what was going on inside me changed my responses. I needed to look at my need for peace. I could see clearly that the out of control, demanding children needed help but it was time before I realised that the very compliant, good children who wanted to please you, also needed attention. They were not learning how to communicate their feelings. They were being praised time and again for being compliant.

These gentle children were getting their needs met, their need to be loved by being the good child. To allow them continue with this behaviour was eventually going to harm them. It is fine to ask a child to compromise in certain situations but to expect a loving gentle child to acquiesce in a situation because another child is creating a scene, is leaving that child vulnerable to being bullied. We began to teach the quiet children how to say no while standing our ground with our more dominant characters and letting them see that they can't have life totally on their terms. When you are tired, or when you are unaware of what it is you are teaching because you grew up with this response it is easy to say, "Do you mind if I give this to Jim or Katie because it will stop them caterwauling." That's what we do. Peace at all costs. Jim or Katie will soon learn that screaming, whinging, or moaning works. Little Mary learns that her needs are not as important as theirs. It might sort out the problem short term but long term it develops into a habit that is difficult to budge.

My problem was never the children. My problem was dealing with adults. I did not have the same emotional freedom with adults. Some parents would arrive before the agreed time. Seeing the small child all ready to play I would be left speechless in front of them. Others were late collecting them. "Liz loves children, so she won't mind." Finding a way to voice my disquiet was not easy for me. That was my next lesson!

Giving in to wants all the time will develop a demanding child who sees his or her happiness dependent on the meeting of this want. No sooner do they get it than they move on to the next one. They become anxious and insecure. Giving in constantly, creates dependence.

When you imagine that you are responsible for another's happiness, clear logical thinking is not available to you

CHAPTER 10

The Dawn of Change

**'The one who would be constant in
happiness must frequently change'**
Confucius

Y EARS seemed to merge into each other. Then change came
without warning. My youngest daughter Annie was born in
April 1988 and at the same time, John saw an opportunity to study
in Trinity College. It was not to be missed. I did not want to put
obstacles in his path. John wasn't happy with his life, that was
obvious. Perhaps, if he had this, then that would be his answer.
There is never a perfect time and this time was no different. I was
not well. I haemorrhaged shortly after Annie's birth from
overworking.

Years earlier I spoke with his father. We were sitting quietly
looking out to the sea drinking a cup of coffee. He asked me to
promise him one thing. I would have promised him anything
because he never asked for anything, so this must have been
important to him. He said he had only one regret and that was not
continuing with education and asked that I would encourage
John in furthering his education.

Fourteen years later I found myself saying to John, "You do not
have to think of us. I will look after our family. You concentrate on
your studies at this time. We will manage". He needed to get into
the mind-set of examinations to pass the entrance exam. It wasn't
easy to concentrate due to general family activities. I found it
difficult to deal with the stress of it all and decided to take the
children in the caravan for a week's holiday until the exam was over.
Annie was six weeks old. It never occurred to me to say, "Can you
go to a library or some other quiet place." This was the level of my
thinking. When you imagine that you are responsible for another's
happiness, clear logical thinking is not available to you. My

nervous system was shot and a sense of urgency took hold. A sense of dread came over me and pushed me forward. Some part of me knew that this was all or nothing. This chance would not come again and if I did not allow it happen then somehow I would have been to blame.

I cleaned and packed the caravan with every conceivable item that would occupy them for the week. I tentatively towed it out of the driveway and through the village. Once on the road I stopped. John followed to see how we were managing. I pulled in and we said our goodbyes. I looked in the mirror and saw him standing there as I drove away. As the week progressed I began to feel unwell. My leg was getting very stiff and painful. I was shivering with the cold though the weather was warm. I went to the doctor when I got home to be told that I had cellulitis. I had to stay in bed on strong antibiotics and not move for at least three weeks. Either I do that or be hospitalised, he said. That threat kept me in bed. The girls were very young and yet they helped me look after Annie. They changed her and brought her feeds to me. Not easy for eleven and eight year olds. I felt resentful that John did not take time off to help. "After all I did for him," was going through my head. I needed him to offer but he was used to me coping. I pretended I was ok. With low self-esteem it takes a major blow to wake you up from accepting the unacceptable. It is responsible for madness because four weeks later we were planning a holiday to England. The doctor said that this was allowable on the condition I rest. We would be staying with family.

On the holiday I managed to keep up the pretence of good health during the day but at night time when the children went to bed I slumped on the couch and promptly fell asleep. The first real chink in my happy marriage illusion came when I overheard a conversation about me and mother-in-law. Prior to this I saw that the only obstacle to our happiness was mother-in-law and that we supported each other with this reality. What I heard was to shatter that illusion. "Does she always sleep like that? It must be very difficult for you coping with Mum AND her." When John answered, "Yes," I nearly passed out. I happened to wake up just as that conversation began. Seeing me as part of his problem I felt betrayed. I had no inkling that he felt that way about me. Mother was a problem being domineering and demanding, but placing me in that category absolutely shattered me. I wept from my soul. I tried my best to put it behind me and put on a happy face and happy family image for the sake of the children but the hurt went deep. I wasn't able to confront either my fear or the problem so I shoved it under the carpet with all the rest of my baggage. We came home and pretended that all was well. I wasn't ready physically, mentally or emotionally to deal with this. Why would I do this? I did it because I needed to believe that all would be well as soon as he did his course!

Though I was gutted by the remark made on holiday I see now that this was the eye opener I needed in order to begin my quest for personal freedom. Without this motivation I mightn't have begun. The seed was planted that there was something wrong with me and the place to look was within me. This was not as clear as it is now but a chink was in place. When we returned to Ireland the acceptance letter from Trinity College was in the post. I breathed a sigh of relief. College was a wonderful experience for him and I knew he was happier than he had ever been before. I put our married life on hold to let him free to do this and I felt that I could deal with the rift when he was in a better position to look at it. What I did not see was that my not speaking about it was avoidance. I thought my inability to speak was tolerance.

Being sole parent to four young children and running a pre-school was hectic. Working with children and living with children with little adult company didn't allow much space for mental stimulation. I was lonely so I threw myself into reading every self-help book I could lay my hands on. My elderly friend Marie Donegan gave me Louise Hay's book "The Power Is Within You". In the meantime, I looked forward to his exams being finished and a time when we could all go on holiday together to Donegal. I did not anticipate that he would feel trapped with us. Basically he had led the life of a single man and to be suddenly immersed in family was overwhelming. I had been hanging in there minding the children and longing for an injection of help. He needed time to adjust and to enter into family life again. I felt suffocated in a small caravan with an energy that I felt did not want to be present. I suggested that he return to Dublin and go back to work and we would stay in Donegal. He could come back to us at weekends. I was uncomfortable with the change but didn't want to be face to face with the reality that was presenting itself. I was seeing the writing on the wall but didn't want to acknowledge it. We had become strangers to each other. We had become incompatible and we didn't have the skills to work it out. No way was counselling an option as he saw this as a form of "bloodletting". Annie was teething and crying quite a bit so at night time I would walk the beach with her to soothe her and me. I needed to breathe in the sea air. Four o'clock in the morning on Knockalla beach in Donegal became my temple of silence. Each Sunday John returned to Dublin on what we christened the Lilac Bus, named after Maeve Binchy's novel. I could sense his relief as he boarded that bus. I'm sure it was as difficult for him as it was for me. The distance was like a wedge between us. I suppose it could be called passive aggressive behaviour on my part in suggesting he return to Dublin without us but I needed space. The notion that this was just a passing phase was gone.

I had no intention of making the same mistake the following summer so when my sister offered us free accommodation and the use of a car in Germany I jumped at the chance. She had been living there for years. We were also given a gift of tickets for two of the children at a time when tickets were quite expensive. Living in a caravan on our own in an atmosphere of tension was not going to happen. In the company of family, I knew the appearance of happiness could be kept up. He was not happy with the idea of going to Germany. The fact was that this holiday would not cost any more than a caravan holiday pushed me forward. What was the problem? It could not be financial. Was the resistance more to do with the fact that for the first time I had decided on where we would go? This was a new development for me. The previous me would have succumbed to the pressure but not anymore. I flew to Germany one week ahead with the children. An apartment in a local village was available for us and we had total independence. This was bliss.

Years later this holiday was to come up as an example of my being a spendthrift. That counselling session was a case of closing the stable door when the horse had bolted. With every passing year the changes were escalating. He wanted me to be strong but as I was becoming strong it proved too challenging. That I would remain the old me so that he could be happy I now knew was crazy. The course was only meant to be for three years but it became five. When the first ended it did not give the qualification that was desired so another course began. I agreed because it could be true. Though I was a bit war weary I could not deny him this opportunity because the same dictum rang out in my head, if he is happy and he sees that I am prepared to support him, then perhaps we could sort out the problems that were raging. The job of single parenting became more difficult. Our son Paul needed a father. I knew we were in deep trouble when I began wishing for October and the new term. It seemed like a stranger visited us for the summer months. Being out of touch for nine months of the year left him behind where we had left off? He was like a pilot flying an aeroplane today on last year's weather chart. I had gotten accustomed to making decisions on my own and the children had gotten used to coming to me to sort out their problems. When John returned, the family dynamic had changed. So much marital pus needed to come to the surface. When the second course was finished another opportunity arose. This time it was a three-year degree course. I had reached my limit. If what was attained could not be put to good use, then another three-year course was only going to be an avoidance mission.

Annie, born when he had begun College was now five years old. Paul needed his presence even more than the girls and it was time he took on that role. So long as the courses remained only as theory in the head then what was the use of doing them? The frustration of his desire to return to college meant that he sat in front of the television in silence. I knew I was not being unreasonable. There was an undercurrent and I could feel it. Resentment built up over time and manifested in small insidious ways, letting me know that he was not happy with me. I remember thinking that if I had to describe these incidences in a court of law an application would have been made for me to go into the home for the bewildered!

On a daily basis it was wearing me down. I remember listening to George Clooney's father speaking on radio. He was talking about how individual freedom was being stripped away under the noses of the American people and they could not see it because each one in itself was not big enough to be worth fighting for. Over time it amounted to a colossal loss of freedom. This slow cooking, passive aggressive way of letting me know that I was out of step was corrosive. I had been under the illusion that I was married to my best friend and that no matter what, we could discuss any problem and be listened to. That in truth was my early perception. I poured out my heart and to all intents and purposes it appeared as if I was being listened to, but when things calmed we were back to stage one again. Nothing changed! I was waking up. Only when pushed to my limit would I speak! By then it was too late. It was greeted with the response that I was just being troublesome. "Am I not allowed to have a bit of peace?" "Why do you always have to spoil a good day?" "We were doing fine until you started?" "Can you not leave it rest?" Whose words? Were they his or his programme?

To outsiders it appeared as if we had the perfect marriage. To us on the inside the situation was completely different. If there was a glaring problem somehow when I brought it up it was turned around as if I were at fault. My explanations were immediately turned on their head and suddenly I was the problem. I do not know at what point of the conversation this would happen but it would and I would be the one at fault. The turn was so subtle that I was not aware of it happening until I was left there speechless. The more I tried to explain my point of view the more the point of view was turned into its opposite and I got entangled in a web of semantics. The mind became so confused I ended up apologising. That feeling of frustration that you have reached another blank wall is indescribable. When you are in the mire you do not see clearly. I wanted the children to have something I did not experience with my father and that was to have a heart connection with their father. The fear that they would not have the opportunity to connect if he continued to study, or the possibility that he might not want to connect, left me trying to find ways to cover up the obvious at that time. I had plenty of theories but no practice in implementing any of them. What was the missing ingredient? It was that I had to change. I was still looking for him to change.

We were on holiday in Achill when I had a dream. In the dream this man is sitting opposite me at a table. He was closed and white faced. I was pleading with him to listen to me but he was stony faced. He refused to engage in any conversation. His face was angry and blank. The dream was very accurate. Unless I faced my demons and let go of what was preventing me from experiencing happiness, I would not experience the peace I desired. The response to what life throws at us is ours. That response will be more painful when we are carrying hurt from our past. We respond through that filter. Judgement and resentment are heavy weights to carry. Band-Aid from books and courses did not get to the root of my problem though they highlighted it. Unless I was prepared to be a witness to my fears and procrastinations, then the insight acquired would not be of benefit to me. I had to face the reality that I did not see me as being good enough. I feared conflict and authority and I was riddled in guilt feelings. These were my demons. I would have preferred if someone else could do the work I needed to do on myself. I read in the book Awareness that through understanding all would change. I would suddenly drop my negative beliefs. The belief that I was not good enough was not going to go away unless I did something about it. Where exactly was I not good enough? Who came up with that idea? Was I prepared to do something about it? What if John changed and used the courses to improve his position at work? What if we were better off financially as a result of his efforts? Where would I be now? Would I be happy if I stayed the same and he changed? I doubt it.

Knowing now that the obstacles I had to move through helped me see that there was a well of talent, ability, courage and strength within me that would not have been available to me if I had stayed in his shadow, has changed my perception of life. There was nothing to forgive. When all the hurt is healed and your system fills up with love, you suddenly realise that the one you saw as your enemy was the one who made you find a part of yourself that was dormant. What if everyone changed to accommodate my fears? Many want that! You change so that I can be happy! That would have kept me in fear prison.

Prior to this I did not see my part in my unhappiness. After therapy it was in my face. I knew I could please no one, not even myself. I had begun to hate myself for being a coward. There was no way out of this mess that I could see. Whereas before I was under the illusion that I could relate to my husband, now I was clearly seeing how shallow it had become. There was no relationship. I talked to him about trivia. If I talked about anything of a deeper nature, he appeared to be hearing me but time told me there was no listening - that nothing was heard. This led to further frustration and depression. All of this was done in an amiable manner.

The word 'responsibility' for our lives was bandied about at all of the workshops and seminars that I attended. To be honest, I never quite got what it really meant. I was being responsible. I was working day and night. I looked after my children. I was doing my utmost to make my husband happy. What the hell were they referring too? In fact, I was over responsible! It took a while before I got it. Every complaint, that someone else was responsible for making me unhappy, making my life a misery, highlighted the truth that my response to my feelings was mine. Prior to this I saw it as another person needing to change. They were responsible for my feelings. If this person is driving me crazy, is the same person driving another crazy? I could excuse it all by saying, "Well it is all right for them because they are not living in my house." The question was, do I change to meet these circumstances and if I do that, do I continue to live in these circumstances?

Where was I choosing to play a victim role? I noticed it through my feelings. It is not easy to accept that the feelings that arise in you are yours and yours only, from your memory bank. Someone else will not have the same response. Which feelings do you wish to entertain? The feelings that keep you down or the feelings that help you move through the challenge? When you are really down and depressed it is not easy to see your way out. It is like being in dense fog. Hardly being able to see your hand in front of you. The inclination is to beat yourself up, to see yourself as a defect? This feeling burned inside me. I was paralysed with it. When I read that I am not that feeling, that feelings come and go, I was not in a position to hear it. You are definitely not your feelings. That I now understand!

This is what Anthony de Mello referred to as detachment. You are not that feeling though it is moving through you. You are not the train that passes through the station at high speed, or a devastating tsunami. Though our feelings can act like the train or the tsunami on our minds and in our bodies we are definitely not our feelings. Like the clouds they come and go. We just have to wait until they do, unless we choose to hang on to them. I could observe what was going on within me when the children were away for the weekend. It allowed me lie there on the bed and watch the clouds of bothersome thoughts and feelings pass. In day to day life as I struggled to make it through the day I had to wait until night time before I could collapse onto the bed and pray for peace. When you are lying beside the person who you see as the cause of your unhappiness it can bring up the feeling of hopelessness. What I did not see was my unconscious manipulations because I feared my own ability to survive. To depend on John to use what he had learned in college, was to place the burden of my unhappiness on him. So long as I did not access my own talents and strengths, I would be unhappy.

I was seen as the giver, the holder of the space to allow him study, but if I am totally honest this was a catch 22 situation. I gave in order to receive. His success was targeted at improving our status. So long as your giving is attached to receiving, you create expectations that may or may not be fulfilled. He gave to me and supported me through College so that he could receive the reward. When I did not return what was expected of me, it brought resentment. There is no blame here but insight into my own neediness.

I saw giving to myself as limited to buying a nice face cream or perfume. I never saw facing my fear as being the greatest gift I could give to me. When I looked back at his College years I felt I had lost five years of my life. I was angry and resentful that all this study did not yield the promise I had expected. I was expecting him to face my fears for me as he was expecting me to face his for him. I can only see this now as I am out the other side and acknowledge the enormous gift in that period of my life. When we expect someone or something to be our happiness we are guaranteed to be disappointed.

Time and again I did not see that I could make small changes in my responses. These are extremely important as they build up our ability to deal with the larger responses. Affirmations did not help me until I was in a position to see where I was going. Looking into a mirror and telling myself that I was beautiful when I had dark circles around my eyes and I looked grey in the face was not helping me. When I saw the way to go, then they were helpful. They psyched me up when trying to move through a fear.

Each and every one of us will find our own response, the response that is helpful to us. I was expecting my children to respond to life through what I thought suited my programme. I am no longer angry with me for trying to programme them in this way but when I saw how this destructive way of thinking affected them, I was. I felt strongly that I wanted them to have a life that was free from the fears I was experiencing not realising that by my own actions and responses to life I was teaching them how to fear.

When in severe difficultly I had a place of refuge. My father-in-law's grave in Glasnevin Cemetery. As my problems centred on family and mother I went to visit him. All through the years my mother-in-law felt it her right to tell us how to live. She was an authority on how I should rear my family. So long as I behaved like the good child all was well. She reminded me frequently how lucky I was to have her son as a husband. She also reminded me that she knew him longer than I and from that privileged position she knew what was best for him. She was adamant that I did not do enough for him and that I indulged the children. She felt strongly that I prevented him from having a relationship with the children. "You," she declared, "do not allow him have a look in," followed by "If you don't mind me saying so..." I didn't want an argument but it might have helped me a lot if I said, "Well, in actual fact I do mind you saying so." I just sat there like a sack of potatoes and didn't respond.

It was impossible to know what to do with her. Guilt feelings, because she was elderly, drew me back every time. All I saw was that if she was not such a major feature in our lives, basically if she joined her husband in Glasnevin Cemetery then my life would be a lot easier! We could all be happy. I look back at that thinking and can only laugh at myself. To wish that she would die so that I could be happy! As soon as she did leave more would come to replace her until I had learned to deal with it. I actually saw her as the total problem.

We had a perfect triangle working for us made up of a Persecutor, Victim, and Rescuer John was victim, as I saw it, of his mother, the Persecutor, I was his rescuer trying to find a way to make peace. So long as we continued to play out these roles then this game continued. Now I can see how harmful this was to us. How could I have respect for him when I was viewing him as being subservient to his mother? How could I not see that instead of taking responsibility for myself, I was expecting him to do my job? I had a problem with this, what was I doing about it and why?

As I sat at the graveside lamenting I felt that I was being disloyal to her. I knew I was not prepared to risk the happiness of the family for her. I was reaching my limit. How could I get through to her about the impact her behaviour was having on our family? Every attempt to stem the tide had failed. She was projecting her image of a successful life on us and we were meant to obey. In her mind we were extensions of herself.

We as parents can easily fall into this trap. What we do not realise is that we are seeing through a filter of our own experience and how we see then can be detrimental to the next generation. When we are busy projecting our images of success, it can be difficult for us to accept that our children need to find their own way and in their own time. Susan Jeffers describes it as "climbing the ladder of success to find we are on the wrong wall." What image of success are we carrying, not realising perhaps that the hearse does not pull a trailer of our earthly possessions to the graveside? The immediate impact of that particular visit to his graveside was a total release from having to please her. The acceptance that I had not got an iota of power to make her happy was in place. I no longer felt the need to stay silent when she was being disrespectful or interfering. That was April 30th 1994.

I had absolutely no awareness of the strength of the bond between my husband and his mother. His words said otherwise.

I felt that one of us stepping outside the triangle would release us to enjoy our lives in freedom. It actually had the opposite effect. As I stepped back, attempts were made to bring me back to the familiar. I had not foreseen the consequences of my decision, not understanding the dynamics fully. By opting out I had changed roles. I was now the aggressor. I did not want to play this game anymore and would not engage.

When the pupil is ready the teacher is sent. I attended a course facilitated by Paddy McMahon, a spiritual teacher and author of many books including The Grand Design and Guided by Angels. One-night Paddy read an excerpt from the book Mastering Sadhana by Carlos Valles. He was quoting the Bhagavad Gita. "Plunge into the thick of battle, keeping your heart at the lotus feet of the Lord. As Arjuna the warrior surveys the battlefield he sees his own relatives standing among enemy ranks. His own cousins and uncles are facing him, weapons in hand, ready for the battle to the death. How can he fight his own flesh and blood?"

I shuddered as he read it aloud. It was a foretaste of what was to come. I asked Paddy if I could borrow the book. I needed to know and understand more. Reading on, I discovered the works of Anthony de Mello. The slow process of real change had begun. What struck me was the sentence, "You cannot make another human being happy." Something has to happen inside them. They have to have a change of mind and heart. You cannot make them change. It is futile. What is worse is that we can feel like a failure because all of our attempts to make them happy have failed. What we do not see is that we see them as flawed human beings. We see ourselves as better. Not easy to have a relationship with someone when they sense that you are on a mission to change them.

Anthony was not saying that you discontinue helping others but you need more discernment. You must to be aware of the kind of help you are giving because it may or may not be helpful. You could actually be assisting someone in staying a victim. To assist a person in remaining a victim is to deprive them of the opportunity to acquire the skills necessary to make their own way in life. Continuing to do too much and your message is that you do not trust this person to be responsible for themselves. This is not abandonment. Perhaps people do not even want your help or need it. No point in you getting angry because you are in full rescue mode. You could be interfering in a person's right to self-determination.

"You cannot make another person love you!" If effort on my part was to make people love me then I would have already been overwhelmed. Instead I seemed to walk around with the name doormat on my back. The more I did, the more I gave, the more I was taken for granted. The Law of Diminishing Returns. If I had no value on my love, time, space or money then how could I expect others to respect me? I had become a human doing and didn't know how to get out of the trap. The compulsive nature of my giving was getting in my way of seeing. I was doing things for my family that they were perfectly capable of doing for themselves.

My understanding of help was actually harmful, the complete opposite of what I desired. What also jumped out from the pages was the blatant truth that though my mother-in-law was a problem she was not THE problem. The bitter truth was that I had a part to play in it all. She could not have interfered in our lives without our permission. Clearly she mirrored to me that any authority figure was creating fear within me and the only one responsible for doing something about it was me. I read somewhere that if you wanted to check your level of spirituality then see how often you got upset each day. Not recognising that I had a problem and that I had to do something about it was like my going to a doctor with an ailment and asking him or her to give me medicine for my neighbour. I had to face up to it. I couldn't communicate how I truthfully felt. It was my level of emotional maturity that prevented me from speaking freely. I could say I tried and I could blame the other for not listening. That could also be true. I needed to witness me communicating. How was it so easy to manipulate me? Somewhere in my illusory mind I thought that if I followed the nice person image then I could bring happiness to the house. That It is why it appeared as if I was the one destroying the peace because I didn't challenge what needed to be challenged throughout the years.

When people were used to my old way of relating, it appeared as if there was something wrong with me. I believed that through understanding alone change would happen. That would not have required me to do anything about it. I misunderstood Awareness. All my problems were going to melt into the background. That the source of our happiness lies within us, is the truth. I cannot do anything for someone who does not wish to access it for themselves. I had to begin on myself. Though many have said, "Weren't you courageous to change?" I often wonder if it really had anything to do with me. Was it that I opened my eyes or that my eyes were opened for me? Timing was not of my making! It was as if we were both heading towards the end of an era and either we walked it together with new awareness or we went our separate ways. Why the sudden, or what appeared to be sudden change? Why was I seeing everything with new eyes? How did this person who avoided conflict at all costs be brave enough to change the course of the river of her life?

To help me continue the process I attended a variety of workshops. In February of 1994 I went to a workshop facilitated by Dr. Christine Page. She took us through two meditations that were to be very insightful for me. She asked us to imagine ourselves in a park and in my park there was a cottage. I was to open the door and see who was inside. I normally have difficulty visualising in meditations but this day I was very clear. I could see me entering a very dark room and in the corner was a very tall person who was bent over. He had no space to stand up as the ceiling was too low. I recognised myself.

The second meditation was to imagine myself as an animal. I

saw a lioness. She opened her mouth to roar but no sound could emerge. She explained the process of change. She said that though many people can see the need for change very few people actually do. She demonstrated this by showing us a door. People do not use the proper exit when wishing for change as they generally continue to bang their heads against a brick wall. What we needed to do was to take some small issue that bothered us and work on that. Something that will not cause too much trouble. Build on change from there.

There were three items on my agenda. I needed to find the courage to confront people who had not paid the fee for their child in the pre-school. Not being able to face them I used the telephone. It was like as if I was the one who owed something and not them. The level of trepidation was out of proportion to the situation.

The next item I felt would not be in any way difficult. The children were getting older and were growing out of caravan holidays so I felt it was time to sell the caravan. When the children were small it was ideal. They loved the freedom and I did too, despite the fact it was a total working holiday for me. The previous holiday in 1993 was a disaster. On that final holiday the stage was set for full on confrontation. What teenagers would want to spend two weeks in a confined space with their mother and father and two younger children? What did not help the situation was that U2 were performing in Dublin and Michelle was convinced that if she stayed in Dublin that she would get a ticket. Tickets were like gold dust. Achill in the west of Ireland is my place for powerful dreams. I had a dream where I saw her climb under a railing and stand in front of U2. She was in the VIP area. She was ecstatic, dancing the night away. I ignored the dream and didn't tell her about it either.

We decided to visit the grandparents' family home in Sligo thinking this would help make up for the disappointment. When we finally reached Dublin on the day of the concert it was too late. She contented herself to listening to U2 on her radio. I went down to my neighbour's house to collect the pet budgies. She said, "You know that Michelle's friend Sarah was looking for her during the week. She had extra tickets for the U2 concert and was hoping to be able to contact her." It was not the era of mobile phones. My stomach heaved. I walked back up the road with the confounded budgies wondering how I was going to tell her. Not only were they U2 tickets but VIP tickets!

I went to visit my friend the next day and told her the story. She said that when U2 started out she used to follow them. On one occasion in Cork she danced on stage with them and Larry Mullen gave her a drumstick he was using. They also signed some single playing records. 'Michelle can have them' she said 'because by the time my children grow up U2 will be long gone!' With drumsticks in hand and the singles I went home to Michelle and told her the story. By then the emotion around missing the concert had worn down and she was very happy to have the gift.

Pay attention to your dreams they have powerful messages. That last episode in the caravan was enough to convince me that we needed to change holiday plans. It couldn't work for them and it was like a living hell for me. So item number two was the sale of the caravan.

The third item on my list was the computer and printer beside the bed. When John came home from college at night he worked there. It was right beside my head. The printer scratched and scraped. I stated in frustration that if I won the lottery the first purchase would be an extension to the house.

Leaving the course that beautiful spring day I felt that the few changes I envisaged would be possible. Nothing prepared me for the reaction. When someone is used to you being a pleaser your change shocks them. You bring up a reaction in them.

It is guaranteed to disrupt the familiar. When change begins, more change is on its way. Stop the deluge before it changes everything was the reaction. I was shifting the goalposts but this time I was not going to put them back to their usual position.

When resistance became strong, for the first time I dug my heels in. I announced that no way in hell would I go on a caravan holiday again. What is more that computer was leaving the bedroom.

My usual response was to go back to my default position of being the nice person. Something in me was not prepared to go down that road again. Peace at any cost did nothing but create an atmosphere of discontent and resentment. Changes to these dysfunctional patterns were creating problems. The atmosphere at home was very tense. Taking this new stance at least had the possibility of positive change. I had also gone for therapy so the old Liz had begun a process of emotional maturation. She couldn't go back even if she wanted to.

I had actually expected encouragement from John. After all he had always been encouraging me to use my talents. He had become so used to me interacting in a certain manner that my change when it came was threatening to him. Expecting a positive response, I became very angry. I know there were times I spewed out that anger. I had no idea just what lay beneath. Only in time did I learn how to hold back until I was clear.

John's reaction threw me. I had spent years blaming others for my unhappiness and I wanted out of that prison. Everyone else was out of step but us and I was used to singing that mantra. Now I saw differently. I wanted out of the Society of Blame and Moan. I did not want to forfeit my new insight because I would have to go back to a state of powerlessness. The person I had expected to support my change was John as he had more to gain than anyone else. I couldn't put all I had learned to good use until I had sorted out my self-esteem issues. He was in the same boat and he too could not use what he had gained in College until he had sorted out his. I saw this as a wonderful opportunity to break through that wall. I flailed about in uncharted waters. I didn't know how to communicate assertively in an appropriate manner so it was like a pendulum swinging in opposing directions. The pent up anger found its expression at various intervals. I was akin to a volcano that had been simmering for years and the resistance to small changes signalled a volcanic eruption. Not being used to venting anger the swing was to return to calm waters. The calm was interpreted as my returning to my senses and so it went on and on until the message was clear that I was not returning to old ways. The predominant feeling was shame. I was not easy on myself, in fact, hating myself for being reduced to what my mother would call a "fish wife." The usual manipulative responses followed

Not one behaviour had the power to get me back to the old me. I had grown up and he hadn't noticed.

Cajoling followed. I fell at this fence because I was briefly taken in by its seeming sincerity. The moment I saw that nothing had changed I was not to be fooled again.

I was very upset during this time. My addiction to approval was forcing me to go through withdrawal symptoms. Guilt was awful. The idea behind my thinking was that I didn't want to hurt people while in actual fact I couldn't cope with being hurt.

I had been accustomed to seeing myself in someone else's shadow. This was to change at Paddy McMahon's course. "Liz," he said, "come out of the shadow! Now is your time." When I really understood what I was reading in Awareness I was very excited. I felt that there were myriad solutions to our difficulties. This I felt we could do together. If we could recognise where our beliefs clashed, where our patterns were from our past experiences, where our fears coincided, then we could find a way. When it was put in such a simple and practical fashion nothing could be easier. If John could see this, then we could be ok. I quoted passages at him. It seemed to do nothing but aggravate him. I needed then to face my worst fear that if John did not want to come on board I might have to face into this on my own. If my friends and family did not want to change, then I had to make my own choices. I was on my own in this. Suddenly Arjuna, the warrior placing his heart at the Lotus feet of the Lord came to mind. The book became my guide. When in difficulty I would open a page and pray for inspiration and guidance. Invariably I would get an answer. When confused I would wait until the mists departed and only then would I take action.

This time my path was different. Once I saw that John was not on board I had to go it alone. I had to just do it. I had to take those small steps myself. With each step I gained miniscule amounts of courage but over time it amounted to a lot. Situations that used to control me no longer had that power. People who had the ability to make me feel helpless, powerless and guilty were finding it difficult to stir these feelings. They were still there but so deep that few people had that power to get to them. Change was finally happening.

I was no longer affected by the behaviours and manipulations that used to control me and bring out of me a negative reaction. Instead I became a witness to my own reactions. Being a non-judgemental witness is important. It allows you choose a different response. This was freedom.

In relation to my children I could see my mother's reactions emerging when chastising them. I was able to choose what was of benefit and what was debilitating to me. In relation to my mother-in-law I could see my helplessness in the face of authority figures. I witnessed that I was passing passive- aggressive behaviours as the desired response to life to my children. It hadn't worked for me and it certainly was not going to work for them. What I also remember was my mother saying and I found myself saying the same, "It costs a fortune to put a smile on that face." I was buying my children's love through doing and spending. They were not any happier for it.

While on the one hand I appeared to be in confrontation with my mother-in-law I was also becoming like her through the years. I had an expectation that my family should fall in line with my perceptions of life, success and happiness whether it was in relation to money, time, or religious views. I was quite a fundamentalist Catholic, and became a Minister of the Eucharist. The way I dressed was becoming more and more conservative. The

Sunday suit was in play. Justification for spending became a way of life, this was my mother's pattern. I had little time for myself and felt guilty if I did. That too was my mother-in-law. There was no social life other than to visit friends or friends visiting us. That too was a pattern. It is quite amazing how conditioned the mind can become. Habits of a lifetime being repeated. What I became conscious of was the dialogue in my mind. I had a permanent Inquisition going on. There was a constant chatter of justification, guilt feelings, condoning, resentment and judgement. Though on the outside people would have looked at me and thought I was a calm person, on the inside this turmoil was going on.

I walked my beloved dog McNabb around Leopardstown racecourse every day. I needed guidance but knew that I could not talk to friends or family. Each one of them would have found it difficult to help or console me. Where I was going in my mind was out of my own mind, away from my usual way of thinking. They were familiar with the old me and as such I needed to go beyond where I had been before.

So began the solitary journey. The unconditional love of my dog kept me sane. I would put my problem to God and then begin my walk. Along the way I prayed for the perfect right action, perfect peace and harmony and perfect solution. I prayed for the highest good for all of us. I did not understand that the way forward was to experience peace no matter what disharmony was in place. There was no easy way out for me. Like most births you have to go through the birth canal alone.

On May 12th I went to Paddy Mc Mahon for a Spiritual Reading. Basically I wanted him to say that all would be well and that my fears of separation were unfounded. I just wanted to know that my children would be fine.

The message I got was to stop being overly concerned for them and to begin looking after myself. He then spoke about my teaching Awareness in the future and that I would write a book. This book, he said, would be my personal journey through awareness and would not a reproduction of Anthony de Mello's or anyone else's book. It would be awareness in ordinary, everyday life. What Anthony de Mello wanted was his work to be used as a tool to help people. He wanted people to drop false ideas of who they are, to drop beliefs that were causing havoc in society and the world so that all beings could be happy and free. This, he said, must happen before we can have true peace. He said that I would find the peace I was looking for through awareness and in time would find that balance between Heaven and Earth.

All that made great sense to me. But I writing a book seemed fictional. I wanted something more practical and I made an appointment to see his partner Maura Lundberg. I wanted to hear the happy ever after story. I needed reassurance. She did not say thankfully, that I would separate but that I was not to be taken in by my husband's apparent approval of the workshops and the reading I was undertaking. She said to take no heed of his words but to observe his body language and the lack of expression in his eyes. This would give me a clearer indication of his beliefs. When you see this, question him on his opinion and it will not take much to bring his true beliefs to the surface. She said that in supporting the family to the extent I was, and my belief that I needed to be fully present all the time, was undermining what I desired most for my children and that was independence. She was right. I believed that I needed to stay at home in order to provide the nurturing my children required so that they could achieve their potential. What I was actually doing was putting a cap on my creativity and in so doing my children were not witnessing a happy mother. I was also doing too much for them and creating anxious children. This belief had the effect of stifling both my creativity and theirs. I told her I was not the creative one that my husband was. He had the ideas. She mentioned my unique gift with children and mentioned that one day I would work with children who had learning difficulties.

Both Paddy and Maura were extremely accurate. What I

loved about both of them was that they did not interfere with my learning process. If either of them knew of my pending separation, they did not say that to me. This was a process only I could go through and only I could decide on. Major steps in your life can only be taken when you are ready and not when someone else says. I found that when I came to a decisive point there really was no choice. It wasn't a question of this way or that way. There was only one way and that was forward. There was only ever one way and it was the way of truth no matter what the consequences. That takes courage and I had to pray constantly to be given it.

I was determined not to share with anyone what was going on within me. It was a waste of time trying to communicate with John as true to that dream while I was in Achill he was stony faced and silent. There was never going to be a discussion. Perhaps he believed I would never go through with it and it was only a matter of time before I capitulated. I could not burden my friends with what I was experiencing because of my fear that I would be hooked into theirs.

My continuing healing meant that we were no longer assisting ourselves in staying stuck. The energy of life had changed between us. When one changes it is as if a light is shone on the other. This makes the energy between them uncomfortable. There is only so long you can wait but can no longer ignore it. When you learn to ride a bike without stabilizers you wouldn't dream of going back to them. It is something like that. Why would you go back to infantile ways when you have moved on from them?

Within weeks the wheels were in motion. The universe must have sent out a message that I was no longer taking caravan holidays. A knock came to the door. "Do you want to sell that auld van, Mam?" The Travellers had arrived. "I most certainly do." "What would ya be lookin for?" I gave my price and he went away. Another group came and the same scenario followed. A game was set in motion. Eventually they agreed on a price and said they would come back and collect it with the money on April 25th. That was Annie's birthday. I had asked them to come at a specific time so that I could go with her to buy a bike for her birthday. She had already looked at one but the condition was that if I sold the caravan she got that particular bike. She was really excited as was I.

No sign of the Travellers on the day. Time was ticking away. I was beginning to feel the pressure. I had promised to take her out of school early at 12.30 pm. I looked at my friend Marie and said, "I am going to pick her up and to hell with them they can come another day if they want. I am getting her the bike." I was getting ready to leave when they arrived. "I'll leave you to it," she said grinning and left. The haggling began. I told them there was no point in haggling because my husband had set a price. That was not going to deter them as they believed they had an easy target. They agreed on the price finally and took out a roll of notes that must have contained a few thousand pounds. By some stroke of genius, they didn't have the correct amount, they needed change and I hadn't any. I told them that they could get change in the local shop.

One of them asked, "Are you a gambling woman?"

I said, "No".

"Go on, take a chance Mam."

They continued for a few more tries and I thought, "Why not?" I wanted out of there in time to get the bike. The shop closed for lunch. They took out a coin. Pitch and Toss. What did I want, heads or tails? They flicked the coin up into the air and as it soared I realised I was conned. They are professionals at this. Up it went and down it came and the only way I knew I won was the expression on their faces. I hadn't a clue which was which. I snatched the final twenty pounds out of his hand and said, "I believe this is mine. Thank you boys. I do believe we have a deal!"

"Would ya not throw in a bit for luck?"

I told them they were lucky to be getting a van at that price. They hitched it up quickly and I witnessed a part of our lives sailing down the road. I got in the car and immediately drove down to the school to collect Annie. We were off to buy a bicycle. The end of an era!

Personal growth has to be that – personal. I cannot be responsible for the growth of another. Each one of us is a participant in our own lives. Going through the eye of the needle to enter the Kingdom of God makes more sense to me now. You can't carry extra baggage and expect to experience happiness.

*I began a process of unearthing
any attitudes I had towards
attracting wealth but also
my attitudes towards my use
of time, space and love*

CHAPTER 11

The Money Programme

'Understanding brings about Change'

Anthony de Mello

B Y sheer chance I saw this workshop advertised. I was sick and tired of barely making ends meet and wanted to create wealth. I thought the workshop would question my attitudes to money and see why I was struggling. What I hadn't reckoned on was a complete and thorough examination of my way of living. I began a process of unearthing any attitudes I had towards attracting wealth but also my attitudes towards my use of time, space and love. They are all governed by the same energy.

This workshop ran once a week for ten weeks so we had time to know one another over the course. As we became more comfortable we helped each other out in the process. Sometimes it was welcome and sometimes challenging!

We were given an exercise to do. There were ten of us in the room as we set about investigating. The exercise was simple enough when the facilitator mentioned it but when I got down to the nitty gritty I found it difficult. I had to write down ten attitudes that my mother, father and some significant other in my life, had to money and finally my own attitude to money.

Finding a starting point wasn't easy. Attitudes? What was the facilitator really looking for? What came were images rather than words.

I could see my mother being nervous around requesting money for essentials. I see her justifying her purchases. I see her fear around money and her dependence on my father.

I remembered her heavy footsteps on the stairs as she made her way weekly for her cheque. Despite changes to the number of children in the household he was not willing to increase the allowance.

I see him driving off in the car without feeling it necessary to say where he was going. He had that freedom. She didn't, asking for the car was like asking for money. She had to justify it. Whatever he purchased was always wise buying, she was seen as a spendthrift.

Whenever she asked for money she was greeted with "Where do you think I'm going to get it from?"

The dominant emotion around money was fear. Dependency created a prison. Never leave yourself dependent on any man was the mantra.

I remember her taking responsibility for clothing the family sooner than ask him. What she could not deal with was the mortification she felt when asking for money. The more I witnessed these images the more I saw myself in them.

It became clear that I was replicating what I had learned from my mother in the way I related to money and to people. I felt physically sick. One participant seeing my discomfort asked if I was all right. He said I looked green. I was. The shock that this was happening to me frightened me. I had fooled myself for years. I believed I was living a new life, not one like hers.

How was I to become free?

I left the workshop and headed for Dún laoghaire Pier. I had to walk by the sea to set my mind at ease before I returned home. Where was I to begin?

The group finished up after ten weeks and another commenced. I needed this support. There were only four of us now. It was during this time I sold the caravan. I was getting brave when I handed over just half of what was received for the caravan and took the price of Annie's bicycle out of the proceeds. The tension was high but the desire to break the mould was even higher. If I followed my mother, then our children would follow us. Something had to give.

The day the caravan was sold was a liberating day. I went to the course and gleefully told them the story. One of my best teachers, Jonathan Philban Bowman, was attending with me. Week after week he tormented me, pushing me to speak out, teasing me, annoying me until eventually I got so angry I broke free of my own self-inflicted silence.

"Finally Ms. Nicey Boots has a voice," he said. I found it extremely difficult dealing with the anger that spewed out of me. I could hear the voice in my head going "Fishwife, washing your dirty linen in public." He was very happy. He wanted me to break free from the debilitating beliefs I had around anger. He was there to heal his own pain, but he was amazing in helping me to heal mine. It is always easier to see where another is stuck.

Another week our facilitator asked us to do a new exercise. We were asked to put a salary on the job of a housewife. We were aware of how much Jonathan was involved in his child's life so we didn't feel the exercise was unfair. He didn't think so either. I thought about it carefully. I could see myself as chief cook and bottle washer. I was painter and decorator, electrician, gardener, seamstress – I made the girls' dresses, curtains, and covers for the couch, I was psychologist, teacher and mother.

My electrical skills were a bit precarious because I thought I had taken out the main fuse before I fixed a light fitting. Thankfully I was standing on a wooden chair with rubber soled shoes because I blew a hole in the knife I was using.

What price do you put on a position that has you on duty twenty-four hours a day? I considered it carefully and decided on my salary. The facilitator went around the group. What is yours, yours, and yours? She then added that this is how much we think we are worth. If she had hit Jonathan with a sledge hammer it would not have had greater effect. How can a stupid exercise like this say that a housewife like her is worth more than me? It was my turn to crow. "Look at it, Jonathan, and see if there is any truth in it." He was so angry. There was no way he could see the fun in this one. Jonathan was one of the most intelligent people I had ever met.

He was extremely talented and we all knew that. This was deeply affecting him and it was time to stop and allow him time to understand what was happening. There was no budge.

Usually I gave him a lift home in my battered old Mini Cooper. He didn't care a hoot whether he got a lift home on an ass and cart or a limousine, so long as he got home. My mini had many defects, one being that the handle on the passenger door was broken and you had to slide the window over in order to get your hand out to open the door. This never bothered him but this night he would walk sooner than come with me. As we were leaving, I remarked playfully, "Imagine me making my millions before you." With a look that shot daggers in my direction he said, "Exactly doing what?" Fresh from my recent success, I said, "Selling tin to tinkers." He looked at me for a moment, then he bent over and laughed heartily. It was great to see him back on form. He was the one person that did not fear upsetting me. I knew too that his tormenting of me had nothing to do with diminishing me. It was a very powerful time.

Anger is simply a sign that you have not recognised the wisdom and the way to take those first steps. You are still caught up in fear and indecision.

Acceptance is the first step out of anger, it means you are ready to see clearly and make new decisions.

CHAPTER 12

Eyes Wide Open

'Things do not change; we change'

Henry David Thoreau

IN to me see! Intimacy.

Digging deep unearthed my insecurities and how they impacted on my life. A cancer undetected is still cancer. Being blissfully unaware that I had any part to play in my unhappiness was just that- unawareness. I was nervous at what was being shown to me in the group. I was afraid of where this was taking me! I often wondered if I was better off living in ignorance. That way at least I could blame others for my unhappy state.

The more I thought about it the more I could hear a voice in my head saying – so long as you are blaming another you are giving them power over your life. You will always be a victim. I couldn't stomach the idea that I was a weak person. I had seen myself as strong, never realising I was just a puppet. The more I saw how influenced, how controlled I was by my own fears the more depressed I became.

This time it was not about changing anyone else, it was about understanding me and doing something about that. It is not a selfish act to live your life as you see fit, it is more selfish that you demand that others live their lives as you see fit. This worked both ways. I could see my demand, my expectations of others that they make me happy. I could no longer expect that of them, but the coin had two sides to it. I couldn't demand that John come with me. He had a right not to change as I had a right to. I could no longer live my life according to the demands and expectations that I remain the old me.

In July, Michelle and Grace were going to visit their Aunt in Germany. My insides were churning and I needed space to digest what I was seeing. My parenting skills were not matching the challenges I was facing and I also needed a rest. My fear of conflict in their early years meant that I was not consistent in my parenting. My peace for peace sake policy meant that the strong were being cajoled rather than being met fairly. I did not have the skills from my own personal experience and I had only begun courses to fill the gaps. When I began working on Awareness my daughter Michelle, with a glint in her eye said to me, "I wish you would go back to your old ways, you were a pushover then."

The night before they left I was helping them pack their suitcases. I sat down for a rest. I felt uneasy about the trip because it was their first time travelling on their own. I was an eternal worrier as control freaks usually are and found letting them out of my sight for two weeks unsettling. I needed to keep their world and mine safe. I was slowly coming to terms with the reality that they were growing up and beginning to leave the nest.

I loved the early years with a passion because I was Captain of the ship and this transition into young adulthood was not an easy stage for me. As small children at least I met their needs as my emotional state was really that of a young teenager, but when they hit teenage years I floundered.

I lay my head back on the couch digesting my thoughts when John entered the room. As he entered, this male voice spoke loudly in my head, "You will separate from this man." The voice was crystal clear. I felt weak to the knees. I could hardly breathe. This was not a conscious thought on my part. I would go so far as to say it was furthest from my mind because fear was not allowing it up into my conscious mind. Though I was being asked questions by the children, 'where is this?' or 'do you know where I could find (some object or other)?', it was like I was on some distant planet. I could not hear them clearly. I had one desire and that was to get out of that room. I made some excuse and went to bed. I lay there panicking and wondered if I was going insane. I knew I heard that voice but how could it be real? I prayed it was only my imagination. I asked to be left alone while I tried to settle myself. Every part of me wanted to break down and cry but I couldn't let the girls see my anguish. Anyway how was I to explain it?

The more I observed the more I saw that my relationship with John was even more superficial than I had felt before. I tried to make it out that this was because of what I was currently experiencing but as I looked back through the years I could see truth. This way of relating had gone on for a long time. I managed to hide it behind daily living. The stress of seeing was painful. As de Mello said, "The most arduous thing you will do in your life is to see." Seeing and accepting reality was more difficult than reading the words in his book Awareness. There was no heart to heart conversations. There was no meeting of minds on financial matters. There was no vision for the future. We spoke of day to day occurrences involving other people but nothing more. "How was your day?" He had little interest in mine as I had in his. We didn't share any hobbies or interests. What connected us were the children and even in that we were not on the same page. How was I to bring the subject up that we needed some form of counselling? The chasm between us was getting deeper and deeper.

The more workshops I attended the more I was seeing and the more books I read on personal growth the greater the chasm. I was not the same person, and it was not possible for me to return to being that old me. Scott Peck in his book The Road Less Travelled speaks on this. What he said was that when only one person attends therapy invariably the other gets left behind. If that person insists on staying out of therapy, then it is almost certain they will part.

Each day I prayed for guidance for some sign, or some action that would naturally bring about a conversation. By October 1994 I knew I had to feel the fear and broach the fact that we were in difficulty. I tried to open the conversation but he stared directly at the television as if I was not present. I turned it off and said that I needed to talk to him about our relationship. I put it bluntly when I said that I feared our marriage was in difficulty. His reply was that I needed therapy. I said that it was because I had therapy that

I was seeing this problem clearly. We had become like brother and sister, not man and wife and that I did not want to continue this way for the rest of our lives. I wanted him to really look at our marriage, to consider what I was saying and that I would give him time to think about this and after Christmas we could discuss it. I was giving him time to see what was happening to us.

The old controlling patterns emerged. In the past these used to have the effect of scaring me but this time it had gone a step too far.

Christmas came and went. Mother-in-law must have had a sense that all was not well because she was the best behaved ever. I was glad of her presence and it was our final Christmas together and possibly one of our nicest. There was no mention of the elephant in the room and shallow conversations continued ad infinitum. Avoidance continued. I knew there was no way this topic would ever see the light of day unless I brought it up.

That knowing angered me. I felt that the dirty work of cleaning this mess up was up to me and no matter how this worked out I would be the one to break the peace. I would be at fault. The burden of this became unbearable and it was the old mantra that emerged. It is better to be hung for a sheep as a lamb. I cannot remember what tipped the balance but it was the last straw. It might only have been a disdainful look, but tip it did. Years of repressed feelings poured out and in the end I just blurted out, "I want a separation, I have had enough. I am not going to live a lie as big as this one. You have not been present in this house for years so what the hell difference does it make? You want me to be as I was twenty years ago. I cannot waste my life like this and I cannot let our children learn that their lives are so valueless that the fears of one person should control an entire family. I cannot have them living life following the patterns of your parents, my parents and us. We have done it up to now, now it is time to change. There is no guarantee that they will not follow in our misery. That, I cannot stand by and watch. I am separating from you and as you have not been willing to even discuss it or look at it I am going to proceed with it. That way you might at least wake up."

"You may want a separation but you can't have it. I will not allow it," he declared. That statement was like an incendiary device. "I can assure you, that you do not have the power over me that you used to," I said. "And you cannot stop me going through with this."

Though the reactions were the usual ones, I felt nothing. I could not believe that I could be so detached. I had changed. I was not that frightened bird any longer. Maya Angelou wrote a book "I Know Why the Caged Bird Sings." That was me for years. Caged by my programme! This was not in any way his fault. That realisation is what made the difference. This problem was within me for years, it had been there since childhood and I was healing it. He too had his childhood problems that matched mine but I could do nothing for him, only he could decide. Doing nothing is also a decision! If he did not see it, then I would have to face my worst fear and go forward on my own. This plummeted him into his familiar behaviours of control, silence, and avoidance and by the time he realised that he needed to do something I was gone, mentally, physically and emotionally. Spiritually I was on a different wavelength. Nothing of the old me, the one he had married, remained.

I had lived with anger, frustration, sadness and despair for a long time. I held on to them for dear life to justify what was happening. That phase was behind me now.

How to come out of this without blaming either me or him! At that stage of my life I was not in that space which made each day a nightmare. Every part of me wanted a breakthrough so that we did not have to go through this but as days passed it was clear this was not going to happen. We continued as if nothing had ever happened. Avoidance and more avoidance was the order of the day. If we ignored it, it might go away. It was like when we were children. "Don't see me," as we prepared to do something we were not supposed to do. There was absolutely no communication. This was the dream I had while on holiday in Achill. This man in front of this lady at a table! She is pleading with him to listen but he is sitting there stony faced. She cannot get him to listen no matter how she tries. She is broken hearted. That was us!

I had no idea what to do next. I went to counselling on my own. It did help to clear my thoughts. I was not asking for major change but some change, even small steps, as a start. Some acknowledgement that we were in difficulty! It came to our anniversary. Maybe this could be an opportunity to salvage something. Nothing! No mention of the anniversary. I sat and watched Shadowlands on the television. I looked at this crusty, elderly English gentleman who was able to change in order to be with the love of his life. I silently wept from my soul. There was no visible sign of any effort to understand.

Mother's day! I got up early. Not a sound in the house. I went for a long walk around Leopardstown Racecourse with my beloved dog McNabb. This was a slow death and I knew it could not continue for much longer. I entered the silent house. No sign of life. I ran a bath for myself and nurtured myself in the warm water. I knew that he was never going to do anything about this and I had now reached a point of no return. At Lunchtime I saw a small box of Lir chocolates on the table. They were symbolic. The children of Lir were exiled for nine hundred years.

"There is no point in continuing with this charade anymore."

"What do you mean?" It was like he was hearing me truly for the first time. By the tone of my voice he knew there was no anger, no frustration or accusation. "I mean we are separating!"

Suddenly he wanted to talk, to get me to change my mind, but I was numb. "You do not have to pretend anymore. Reality is we have drifted apart. We are not the same people and there is nothing you or I can do about this. I am not asking you to change anymore. I don't want that for you, because you do not want it for yourself. But you cannot demand that I stay the same as I used to be. That person is dead and cannot be brought back. It is best we separate because we are very different people now. To bring the children up in this environment would be harmful. I am doing this for the sake of the children though everyone seems to think that we should continue to indoctrinate them in old ways. I cannot do this. I haven't the strength of will to do this for me but I most certainly have it to do this for them."

With that he left the room. For the first time he knew that I truly meant it. This was not an idle threat. There was no way I wanted to teach my children that it was perfectly normal to slide out of personal responsibility in relationships. Burying our heads in the sand was not going to be an option.

He said he would go for counselling. As I had been used to promises, I now wanted to see it followed by action. I gave him the number. The following day I saw the number in the gutter. I handed him the number and mentioned where I had found it. He went to counselling but told me it was all too simplistic. I kept praying that I would be shown if he was making some effort to save our marriage. I answered a telephone call from the local library. They had a book available for him on how to clarify one's monetary rights during separation. What were the odds that I answered that call? He shifted uncomfortably when I said that the library had a book ready for him. I had to take it a step further. I needed to close the playschool. I would not be reopening it the following September. Funnily enough it was also the first year we were not booked out in advance. After fourteen years it had come to its natural end.

I went to a solicitor for advice in June. We went through everything and she helped me make out a deed of separation. Though I knew he would not pay attention to this through fear, I also wanted to shock him into actually doing something to save the marriage. The letter arrived and I could see it sitting on the hall table unopened for days. There was a major part of me hoping that something would change, yet each time I went down this road of thought some other awakening happened.

On August bank holiday, in an effort to pretend that life was normal we decided to bring Paul and Annie to the beach. It was a beautiful day, not a cloud in the sky. It was also crowded. We found a place suitable for the children. He placed the rug on the sand and lay there looking sad and miserable. I sat and observed the children playing happily. How could this be right? How could breaking up a family be the only way out? Am I being selfish and delusional? I sat looking out to sea and prayed from the depths of my being. "God, if this is right show me a sign. I want to see it in bold capital letters. Nothing short of that is acceptable!"

With that a young boy stood in front of me. He was blocking the sun and my view to the sea. I wanted him to move and was about to ask him when I noticed what was written on his t-shirt. JUST DO IT. I was stunned. I was frightened that what I had asked for, bold capital letters were put in front of me. My mouth went dry, my body tense and I wanted to get as far away from that beach as possible.

The deed of separation requested that he leave by September. I knew he could live with his mother because she had always said that she had his best interests at heart. She was never going to abandon him or he her. Michelle was going into her final year at school and the pressure of this could not continue. We needed some form of resolution. When we got home I asked, "What arrangements have you made for leaving?" The air was dense. Reality hit home. Some way had to be found! Something had to happen.

Throughout this summer I continued to attend The Money Programme. We were like the three musketeers by that time. By virtue of the small group it was not possible to hide from them what was happening and though I did not speak directly about my situation all knew I was under extreme pressure. Whenever I sought advice I felt even more pressurised by the opinions of others. This was a road only I could go on and I needed to be in a totally different space to make truthful decisions.

It was for this reason I spent a lot of time on my own in nature, in total quietness. Only with a quiet mind could a solution be found. There were times the internal chatter went on nonstop. There was no switch to turn it off especially when surrounded by daily activities. It was sheer terror. When on my daily walk I sat under a tree and allowed my world to stop. McNabb sat beside me sometimes licking my face. My faithful companion. I knew that my trying to analyse situations over and over again was not helping. As often as I could I made a conscious effort to quieten the mind.

It was only as a result of that practice that I was able to hold fast to truth. Whatever decision I made, it could not come out of fear! I had one more class on my Thursday nights and only Jonathan turned up. Our facilitator Patsy Brennan suggested we go to a local pub for a bite to eat. Jonathan was in rare form. He questioned me up and down as to what was happening to me. He then began to speak as if he were the local parish priest in a John B Keane play. He spoke in perfect mimicry of the Kerry accent on the reasons why I shouldn't leave a good man, who neither bate me nor drank. The more he continued the more mesmerised I became. He was coming at me full tilt with ideas and suggestions as to why I should continue with such folly. He kept this up for a considerable time and then abruptly stopped and looked me straight in the eye.

"And do you know, girl, what the solution is?"

I asked him, "What is the solution, Jonathan?"

He said, "That is where he has you hooked, you haven't quite made up your mind yet. Every time you think you are clear he throws a hook and snares you. It is clear there is no honesty in this relationship and if it hasn't happened by now it is not going to happen. You and only you have to decide if you want to stay or leave this relationship that is clearly toxic, but that is not for me to decide. You are on your own in this. Do you feel you can live out your days with him? Can you live with the truth that you are teaching your children that it is honourable to live a lie?"

Jonathan could not be anyone other than Jonathan. I knew he

would definitely not intentionally harm me or anyone else. I also knew if he saw me lying to myself he would give it to me straight. I am indebted to him. Every step I took I prayed. I prayed for the highest good of all of us, John included. Every question I asked I got an answer that pointed me in the direction of separation. I had to trust that.

Damien, one of our best friends, was dying of cancer. I was going through my own private hell and I did not want to burden him. I kept away for some time because he had enough to be dealing with. The week before he died I had a feeling that something had changed and went to visit him in the hospice. He was all tied up with tubes and was asleep. I sat there and waited with him quietly until he woke naturally. He said he knew I was there but did not have the energy to speak. I asked if there was anything I could do and he said he would love to visit the gardens. I tried to lift him into his wheelchair and to manoeuvre the drip. I could see how frail he had become as I put on his socks and tried to hide my tears that fell to the floor. As we made our way through the door, not being used to wheelchairs I hit the side. He laughed loudly and said, "This is great; they will be able to say I didn't die of cancer, she f******g catapulted me through the door!"

It lightened the occasion somewhat and we set off. I allowed him be the guide as he knew the place better than me and he insisted on taking me past the mortuary. He commented as he saw a funeral cortege heading towards the chapel, "This week some poor sucker, next week me." I kept my head down and kept pushing. I sat down on a wall and we talked. He asked why I had not been to visit him. So I came clean and told him about our difficulties. "I wish you had told me sooner. I thought I had done something to upset you." I wish I had too but somehow in talking about it, it made it more real. I told him how grateful I was to him for introducing me to alternative therapies. "Do I have to die so that you can live in truth?" he stated with a grin.

Damien's death left its mark and pushed me to live life fully. He died a week later. His death was a reminder that if it is possible to make changes, they ought to be made quickly.

Some weeks later I was asked if I would attend Catholic Marriage Counselling. I had little regard for the limited understanding the church had for marriages in difficulty. I could not see that this would be of any help but I agreed to go. I asked that I see this lady on her own first. I spoke truthfully to her about our lives together and why I wanted this separation. She was completely taken aback. The stories did not match. I told her I had nothing to gain from lying to her; I was just placing truth on the table. She then requested a joint meeting. Short of a miracle there was no way I was returning to a fake marriage. It was like that film, December Bride. Keep everything smooth to the eye. What will people say, what will people think? It doesn't matter that you are deeply unhappy so long as society approves of you.

My usual response when under threat is to defend myself, justify why, and get verbal diarrhoea in the process. I was too tired for that and allowed him speak.

I needed to hear what was happening in his mind. I hadn't heard it up to then. He never divulged anything. So now was his opportunity. It came as a deluge. I had no idea he held so much resentment towards me for so many years.

This was not a recent thing. The difference was that this time it was verbalised. The counsellor too was quite clear that the problem was not recent. As I described my way of living and reacting to situations as a young twenty-year-old she could see how over the years this was magnified. It had only come to a head. As there was no willingness to address it, it kept on keeping on. It was incremental!

November came and my sister offered me a week's holiday in Germany. I travelled early December. I thought that if I was out of the house and away it would give us both space to reconsider. A friend drove me to the airport. On the way I told her what was happening. I only mentioned the pending separation to a few. She was flabbergasted. As she put it, "Of all the people in her circle she never would have thought our marriage would end up on the rocks." No one knows the truth of another's unhappiness.

I flew out on Sunday. While there, my sister insisted that I avail of their medical services. They had a clinic and it was easily done. I resisted at first as I felt too tired and didn't want anyone poking or prodding me. Eventually I relented. I had the space to detach from what was happening to us. When I saw how John behaved as if nothing were happening, I had absolutely zero sympathy for him then. It was all words, no love there. When the Universe wanted to inform me of reality it found plenty of opportunities. We just have to listen and pay attention to what is being shown to us. I prayed to be shown and I most certainly was every step of the way.

On December 28th my sister telephoned with the results of the tests. She didn't want to phone before Christmas that I was in serious trouble. The smear test had shown up anomalies. In fact, a friend of hers with a better result than mine had recently died of cervical cancer. I was told to do something immediately. I had a sinking feeling that it was expected I would call off the separation show. The threat of full blown cancer made me even more certain that if I had only six months to live I wanted them to be happy. I wanted to be able to place my head on a pillow and be surrounded by my children. I had to be clear. If I continued with a meaningless marriage I had a greater chance of developing full blown cancer. That I was not prepared to do!

Do not fear life; fear your lack of courage to embrace all life. Observe how you become an emotional slave to the person or situation that you think is controlling you. Start by becoming aware of the thoughts, that either keep you in the past or the future.

CHAPTER 13

The Leave Taking

**'Are you willing to be sponged out, erased, cancelled,
made nothing? If not, you will never really change'**

D.H. Lawrence

NO one chooses separation lightly. Choosing a path for you though difficult is not the same as choosing one that also involves four children ranging in age from seven to eighteen. That each one was to be deeply affected was without doubt but in my heart I knew if I did not choose this way ultimately the price for them would be too much. Once I saw the necessity of evolving, of rooting out old beliefs and habits I knew that I had to pave the way for a new way of living life.

Knowing what I understood then about toxic relationships, it was imperative that I should do this. If there had been a way to communicate feelings honestly, if they could have been listened to and respected, if change was possible within the marriage, then to stay would have been less disruptive and, less painful, for the children. Many thought I had made a conscious choice and was relentless in its execution. To me when it all came down to the essentials there was actually no choice between this way of life and that, there was ultimately only one way. Going back to old habits and dysfunctional patterns was not an option.

Robert Rowland Smith wrote an interesting observation about separation. The question was, is it better to leave or be left? Relationships he suggested initially are never symmetrical. Being left is horrible, but you don't bear the responsibility borne by the leaver, or do you? Unconsciously the person left often agrees to the separation, and may even have provoked it. So perhaps symmetry prevails. Silence and inactivity also have a role to play!

Children absorb every nuance in their living environment; they absorb our habits, beliefs and behaviours and may not recognise them in themselves until much later in life. It enters their memory bank. I was recognising where my past was destroying not only my present but theirs and in healing my past it had to have positive implications for them. When I separated it was for my children. Without children I could have gone back into the world of work and coped that way. It might not have been the life I had hoped for but with an independent income I could have camouflaged my feelings or so I thought. What we were both passing on was too dysfunctional yet with the threat of cancer in the air the almighty fear was whether I would be alive to carry the children through. Secretly I hoped he would come to me and say that he loved us all so much he would be willing to really look at our relationship and commit to change. Very little would have done me at that time because the prospect of my bringing the children up on my own while going through the trauma of separation and health issues, was monumental. I was not asking for an awful lot. I wanted transparency. I wanted to be a wife treated respectfully and with equal status. I had fooled myself for years into thinking that this was so. Reality was different. You hear lots of loving words. They confuse you into believing they are true. Yet when there is no positive action with the words they are like empty vessels. Hollow! You are not able to love freely when your subconscious mind is overloaded with hurt feelings.

I knew something was afoot before Christmas. Some things went missing from the house. They were only small things but indicators that movement was happening. Life was in slow motion and each day was painfully gotten through. Whenever I doubted my decision and weakened, I was shown a behaviour, an action, to let me know that nothing had changed. I felt like a traitor, the betrayer, the one who destroyed. I did not know when the move would take place but knew it was coming down the tracks.

As he packed upstairs we all sat in an uneasy silence by the fire in the sitting room. Annie played in a cardboard box that was left in the hallway. She pretended it was a boat and lay in it imagining she was on the ocean wave. Ironic because she has always hated boats! Anger and rage blinds us! Unawareness and ignorance cause havoc. Whatever empathy I felt was emptied out of my system that evening. Whatever anger he had towards me for catapulting him into being responsible for his life and for his own happiness was understandable, but I could not take responsibility for his decision to bury his head in the sand.

I see me then still maturing and a long way from home. Handling this situation through hurt feelings with little skill for communicating created the very atmosphere I always dreaded. Though I was showing courage and strength, that courage was still not rooted within me and I acted as if everything was fine and I was in control. I believed that once he left life would get easier because this drip, the drip of uncertainty that had gone on since 1994 was dreadful.

I did what I always did in a crisis I turned to comfort food. We ordered pizzas. That was a luxury. It was how we coped. It was like circling the wagons as we huddled together. I barely slept that night and as morning came I stared at the bedroom wall. I looked at the wall like Shirley Valentine and said, "Is that all there is to life?" "Is this it?"

That wallpaper had been there since 1981. This was January 1996. I saw a piece turned up at the corner and I ripped it off. The tear made this fantastic sound. I quickly got into the rhythm of it and before long sheets of it were all over the place. I opened the windows to let in fresh air and continued the task. The ripping noise woke up the girls and they came in to see what I was doing. I said, "I have to make this room different. I am suffocating. There is one tin of paint in the shed left over from painting the hall and it will do for now. "Can we change ours, too?" "I don't have the money to buy the paint," I replied. "We have our Christmas money; can we buy it?" I had no problem. I went and got colour cards from the hardware store and we sat down to choose colours.

Paul and Annie were sad to be left out of this and they too said that they would love to change the colours of their bedrooms. Again, they used their own pocket money from Christmas. If this helped them through then this was the way to go. Each one in their respective rooms preparing for change! As we all worked quietly away he walked into the house, took some items and walked out slamming the door. How it looked from his perspective I do not know. It must have appeared as if we were having a celebration. Painting was therapeutic for the moment. Each one of us would have to heal ourselves in time.

I had worked in a bank and luckily I always kept a separate account. Housekeeping money was transferred into it and it gave me a semblance of independence to keep it this way. I had no income now as the play school was closed. When I had my pre-school I didn't ask for extra as the size of the family grew. My mother's pattern.

I attended a Reiki Masters course and thought that I might be able to do some healing work. I had enough going on to heal myself. There was little energy available to do anything much for anyone else. One lady used to come to me on Friday's. I got twenty pounds. We used that as a treat. A bale of briquettes for the fire, club orange to drink, a video and chocolate Hobnob biscuits.

I had my Mini Cooper. It was a 1969 model and was not suitable as a family car. But I loved it. When we went to our local shop I had to ask the children to get out before we went over the ramps because the sub frame was too low. This was a source of great amusement for us. It was inclined to be temperamental! Some wet days it would start up fine and on others it wouldn't move. What it could do was go through snow because it had front wheel drive. This was a godsend because Paul was taking part in the musical Bugsy Malone that January and he needed to be present for rehearsals. We moved up those hills as if there was no problem. It lasted for the duration of the musical before breaking down. I telephoned our usual mechanic to see if he could help and was met with silence. The beginning of the departure of many people I had considered friends had commenced. I had to find a new mechanic! When you hit hard times, especially when the entire world around you is in boom, you quickly find out who is your friend. The people I thought would be with me departed and others that I would never have expected would be sympathetic were supportive. Marie who worked with me and her husband Bill gave me one hundred pounds. They had no idea what this gesture meant to me.

Tommy lived next door. He was definitely what we would call "the salt of the earth" and a friend to us both throughout the years. From the word go he said that if ever I needed something not be hesitant to ask. I knew that I would if there was an emergency but was so grateful for the words that I cried openly in front of him. His help was always discreet. It was always given unconditionally and with a fulsome heart.

One day I was out mowing the back garden. It was a huge garden and the lawnmower was nearing its end. I had various means of convincing it to stay alive but this day it gave its last. The grass was so long and as the garden had been my pride and joy seeing it this way distressed me. The engine died and nothing could bring it to life. Perhaps Tommy heard my efforts or maybe he saw me sitting at the side of the house with my head in my hands quietly crying in despair. Later that day as I composed myself I went out to the front for a walk and he met me. "Liz, if ever you need a loan of my lawnmower, please feel free to ask for it. It is there for you." Throughout this time, it was never big gestures that mattered so much but the small acts of kindness that kept restoring my faith that I was being looked after.

Each one of us did what we each had to do. Having children means you must get up and go through the process of each day. They need that. They were also amazingly supportive despite the fact they too were going through their own grief. They wanted and needed their father's love. They wanted him to show it to them.

The car broke down in great style and we had nothing. The weather was not helpful in that it seemed to rain constantly or perhaps it is how it appeared. Grace and I went to do the shopping and we carried it home. She was not going to allow this defeat us. She made me laugh the whole way home with her quirky sense of humour. Having a sense of humour transforms the most testing times. I had to get rid of my lovely Mini Cooper. Selling it was akin to putting a pet down. I found a buyer and did a trade in for a piece of scrap that functioned well for two years. It bided time until I could get something a bit better. I was living in fear each day working on permanent adrenalin. Nothing had been put in writing, no agreement had been made, and no communication. Each month I would check to see if the housekeeping money had been put in. This was no way to live. I also had an appointment with the gynaecologist to see what lay ahead for me.

I discovered that we had mediation services in Ireland available to people to help them through this time. There were people available who would help you sort out finances and who could formulate a separation agreement with you and in essence cut out the need for any court proceedings. I made an appointment with the agency and asked if they could help us. They set up the meetings and with trepidation I headed in. I felt that with a third person present this would be very helpful for us both. I was hopeful going in. I met with a brick wall. We could not get past his belief that as I had initiated the separation then it was my full responsibility. He could not see any reason why he should be responsible when I had opted out of the marriage. She wanted to find ways to help him develop an independent relationship with the children. Anger blinds us.

Three sessions in and still not one budge in any area. Still the same argument, why should he engage when I was the instigator of this breakdown! On my fourth meeting I happened to drop in to a restaurant in Westmoreland St. It was owned by one of the participants on The Money Programme. I sat quietly and had a coffee with him and told him what was happening. He said, "Liz, two things you can do. Number one, go to the tax office and get single parents tax free allowance. He, too, is entitled to it should he decide to take the children for an overnight stay. This will also ensure that he spend the time that he wishes to have with his children. The second is that you go to the District Court and you get a court order for maintenance that the mediator decides is fair and have the court direct this order to your husband's workplace."

This meeting was our last attempt at a breakthrough. I hoped I would not have to make this ultimatum because if this failed, I would have to go down the legal route. All the time I was wishing for some miracle not seeing that the miracle was me standing up for my rights and the rights of the children. Standing up for truth!

Truth can be misunderstood. I could look out on the greater world and see its absence but not see it in me. Only when in counselling did I see how much he had withheld from me his true feelings through the years, but also how much I too had withheld from him. Neither of us was being honest. Now I was confronted with the truth of myself. I had lived a lie. He didn't make me live it. This I did to myself in unawareness. I did not know I had courage until faced with this. I was being pushed to speak out. John was making me walk my talk. He was making me live awareness. While I was praying for an easy way out, I was also praying for the highest good of us all. That being so, I also had to accept that this challenge was of benefit to us all. He was also being allowed to see what was preventing him from his own happiness if he wished to see it.

I went in and sat down and waited as this lady did everything in her power to bring about some compromise. She met me in the hallway. "I have never mediated with a couple before where absolutely nothing was achieved. This is a first for me." I told her I understood but it also gave me comfort that I was not imagining that I had hit a brick wall. This was it. I looked over at him and said, "That is your final decision." "I don't see any reason why I should be responsible for your actions," was the reply. "Well at least you are clear. Now can I make myself clear? I am heading to the tax office to get single parents tax free allowance, and when that is done I am heading straight to the District Court and there the Judge will decide on a maintenance order and it will go to your Personnel Department .I am out of here now," and I picked up my bag to make a move. "Nothing that has been documented here can be used in court, I hope you understand this." said the mediator. I said I did because in my initial interview this was pointed out to me.

When anger arises you have a choice. There is a gap between the reaction in your body and your response. You can choose the response. The reaction comes from your pain; your response can come from insight or pain. Only when you become familiar with what is happening in your body can you make that choice.

I got a letter to say he had changed his mind and that he would continue with what he had been giving up to that time. This would not be enough because Michelle was doing her leaving cert and she would need help if she were to get a chance to go to College. The years the children were facing were going to be expensive ones and something had to be put in place to ensure they were looked after.

I had more medical tests done and needed hospitalisation immediately. I sat in Bewley's Café one evening with my friend Felicia. She was in good spirits because she had been financially rescued having inherited a large sum of money. So it was free coffee and sticky buns all around. We chatted for some time and then she looked me straight in the eye. "You haven't decided whether you want to be here or not?" Thinking that she was referring to my being in town with her I looked at her quizzically and asked "What do you mean by that?" "I mean on the planet," she said. "You are beaten at the moment and before you go for this surgery make up your mind where you wish to be." Was there some truth in this? I knew there was. This sharpened my wits. I most certainly did wish to be around and having taken the children out into the open I had to be there to continue what I had started. The date came for the surgery and I prayed that I would make a full recovery. I also prayed that he would not come anywhere near me because being so vulnerable I might weaken. I am one of the lucky survivors. My time wasn't up yet!

It took a little while to recover and what helped was the generosity of people with their time or their gifts. Some massage therapists offered massage, one gifted me a reflexology session, and another allowed me attend her workshop. It kept me involved with others who were also searching for some meaning in life. One such person was Gemma. She was very down to earth. Many who are involved in healing are up in the clouds but she was definitely not one of them. She said, says, "The bottom line is that you are going to have to put bread on the table. Forget about Reiki and healing, work with what you are trained to do. You are a qualified teacher. Make out your CV and go back into the workplace!" It was the one place I did not want to return to because this was the choice of my mother-in-law. I didn't see it as my choice. I very quickly realised as my own mother would say "Beggars can't be choosers." I wasn't getting sufficient work in Reiki so I went over to my elderly friend Marie and between us we made out my CV. I began to get some substitute teaching work. It was difficult initially getting back into the swing of teaching but seeing that cheque come in made such a difference. Not getting it for the months of July and August showed me how important it was to get more CV's out there for the autumn.

Life goes on and Annie's First Confession and Communion and Paul's Confirmation needed to be acknowledged. She was finding it difficult to understand the whole idea of a First Confession. In her mind she had no sins. In my mind she also had no sins. I had to go to a meeting in the school to meet the priests and other parents. The priest asked, "What has changed since you went to your First Confession?" So many came out with these lovely lofty ideas of change that I found it impossible to stay quiet. I said, "There is no change; there is plenty of camouflage but no change."

"How can you say that?" he enquired. "This is how I see it and how Annie sees it. In my time we were told to invent sins for that First Confession," I replied. I was terrified the sins I had to tell were not good enough so I had to embellish them. I told the priest I had cursed thirty-six times and that I stole apples and I had dirty thoughts. I hadn't a clue what dirty thoughts were but in discussion with the others in my class we came up with them. Now here she is and what she is being told is to invent sins."

"Of course she has sins!" he said, "You can make them simple." Then he added, "You can say, she was disobedient when she didn't help Mammy. "This further added fuel to my fire. "If she doesn't help Mammy and runs out to play surely it is because me, Mammy has a problem in getting her in." My friend Catherine whispered to me, "Be quiet or we will be thrown out, you for challenging them and me for being with you." She was quietly laughing. The subject was changed. I continued, "Has Annie the right to go and be blessed without having to invent sins? If that is the case, then there is change. If not, then no change." I got no response.

Annie told me not to worry because she was inventing a few of her own to make him happy. Conditioning! The night of the First Confession was a beautiful evening. The ceremony was to be in her school. She skipped ahead of me holding Grace's hand as they walked by the river. They played just a little Billy Goat's Gruff over the bridge before we continued our journey to the school. The school always put on a lovely ceremony. The girls' choir sang hymns that would bring a tear to the eye. Annie sat nervously between us both and when it came to her turn she bolted out like a little fawn. She sat there and had a happy conversation with the young priest who admired this little soul so much. She came down, relaxed and took her place in the middle of us. It was a lovely memorable night.

She didn't want to wear a dress for the First Communion. I suggested that if it were possible could she wear a white robe over her denims. She was happy with this and our young Fr. Paul told me he admired the way she was true to herself and he had no problem with it. The week before she said, "Mum, I will wear a dress and be like the rest of them!" I took out my sewing machine and began a labour of love. I made a dress that I knew would look beautiful on her. It was simple and chic. As she approached the altar she lifted the dress to allow her room to climb the steps and as she did people noticed her basketball socks and trainers. As one mum put it, "Seeing the trainers I knew that Annie will always be true to Annie." She was.

The effort to keep emotions under control on these family occasions was very difficult. The tension was enormous because they were the first main family occasions since separating. We got through it somehow.

Summer came and one night a week I attended a course called Expressing Yourself as Woman. Margaret Neylon was the facilitator. Margaret was full of life, wisdom and understanding. She had the happy knack of drawing the best out of us. There is no doubt that she was a catalyst for many people and she connected us all in many ways. It was in this group I met my very good friend Kate. Both of us were going through challenging times and we had many common interests. It was during this time that I had one of my breakthrough experiences. I lived off my overdraft and knew that I had to make peace with my bank manager before I bought the school uniforms and books for the coming year. He agreed to allow the extension knowing that I had some chance of work in the near future. I went into town with all the book lists and queued like so many others on the street outside Greens' book shop, until I had everything needed. The bill was enormous as it normally was.

On the way home I decided to treat ourselves to a beautiful meal. I went to the shopping centre and filled the trolley with food that each of us loved. I went to the check-out and put it through, handed over the card with confidence and waited and waited as the girl tried to process it. She handed me back the card and told me it was declined. I nearly fainted. I said, "There are funds there; I do not know what has happened." This was before ATMs and it didn't occur to me to write a cheque. Anyway she might not have taken a cheque after that fiasco. I left the trolley there and went out to the car. My stomach was sick. The kids had to be fed for the weekend so I called to a friend to help me. I got a lecture. You will need to examine your expenditure. We need to see your outgoings and your income and see where it is you are overspending. "Oh my God, I came for help and I get this." How was this in any way helpful? Perhaps another day, but when you are living on the clippings of tin, a lecture to see whether I was spending on luxuries is not what you want to hear. Eating humble pie, I accepted the money and went to the shops. With a heavy heart I put the key in the door. I felt so burdened I couldn't speak to the children. They were quite excited with the new books and clothes so I excused myself and went to lie down. "What was happening? What was I meant to learn?" Then I saw it. Here I was again taking full responsibility for the children's expenses.

I decided to go and visit John the next morning. I met with the usual response. "You chose this, so you are the one responsible." I kept it up, "They are also your children and you are responsible for half of what it costs to send them to school." I quietly kept up the mantra and I got it. I had to move through my resistance because every part of me wanted to bolt out of the place and say to him, "I will pay for it myself rather than demean myself in this way coming to you with a begging bowl." Then I realised that reaction was my family legacy. That was what my mother did and she suffered and that was what I did and I was suffering. I needed my children's love. My playing the martyr role meant that I thought I was getting it. With awareness I saw how selfish this was because it created distance between them and their father and ultimately I would lose out because children get fed up with being controlled by guilt. "After all I did for you". Playing the martyr was conditional love.

This lesson was the beginning of many more to come. There

was no shouting just passive resistance and yet this was always enough to get me to back off before. I looked at him kindly and said, "One day you will thank me for this." "I very much doubt it," he replied. I left feeling much better about myself and with the knowledge that I did not have to be always the one to pick up the tab. Though it never got any easier for me as old habits die hard, I still followed through until it became a natural response. Subtraction of negative beliefs about ourselves assists us in all of our relationships. That process allowed him the freedom to build loving relationships with all of his children. He was part of their lives. If I had taken over, the outcome could have been different. The insistence on my being the good person could have damaged their relationship with him and me.

Monday came and with trepidation I went to the Bank. I spoke to the same bank official and he went through the account. He looked baffled. He came to me and apologised. I do not know what happened because not only did you have the overdraft facility which covered you but your maintenance came in late. I had not seen this on Friday because like a rabbit in headlights I just asked for the overdraft facility afraid to look at the actual balance. I smiled at him and left. I felt the Universe has a peculiar way of letting us know where our greatest learning lies.

My definition of a nice person was out of focus. To me a nice person was one who did not make any waves. Not causing waves means you are the one to back down which ultimately may not be good for any party concerned. Allowing this to happen over the years, accumulated into a major cop out for both of us! My not challenging the system meant that our marriage was allowed to stagnate unquestioned for all those years. Though I had made some attempts, the attempts were through the nice person image. There was no substance to it.

Years later I would see this but through the eyes of a child. I had a small group in my class. One young girl was getting herself into difficulty playing cupid games with young boys. I was explaining to her that she could always say no to the advances of these young bulls. "I do Miss, I do be tellin' them to go away." I wanted to hear more and asked her, "Mary, when you are saying no, are you smiling at the same time?" "Yes, Miss." "Then to them Mary your answer is yes." Saying no and then adding a sweetener dilutes the message. This applied to me also.

One Sunday afternoon Grace and I decided to go to an open day in The Healing House, Phibsborough, Dublin. I was immediately drawn to Cait Branigan and her work as a Shaman and Reiki Practitioner. This was the beginning of a significant relationship. Cait helped me identify childhood trauma and how it played out in the present. It was through Cait that I was able to complete the jigsaw of my role in acting out dysfunctional patterns in relationships. Her insight when I was at my lowest was necessary. What she did was to help me understand more fully my relationship with myself. She helped me see how fear operated in my life. This was important for me as I was making my way slowly out of the mire. When you are in new territory it is easy to be dissuaded from a path that is right for you. Cait never interfered, never told me what to do but was the perfect sounding board. She understood my need for the highest good for all concerned. She also understood that sometimes the highest good is also the rocky road.

Enlightenment comes slowly!
Subtraction of negative beliefs about ourselves assists us in all of our relationships.

CHAPTER 14

Keep on Keeping on

'If error is corrected whenever it is recognised as such, the path of error is the path of truth'

Hans Reichenbach

THE long summer with no work left the coffers depleted. September came and I felt that surely there would be some work. The phone was silent. A friend was heading off on the holiday of a lifetime. She was cashing in her life insurance policy. I thought of mine. I had taken it out before a gallbladder operation in 1984. I was terrified that if anything happened to me there would not be sufficient funds to look after the children. I telephoned the insurance company nervously and was told that since the policy was only in my name I was the only one who was authorised to cash it, even though I was not the one paying the monthly instalment. I couldn't believe my good fortune. He told me it was very little. "How much is very little?" I asked. "Two thousand five hundred and sixty-five pounds," he replied. To me it was a small fortune!

Every step of the way something happened exactly when we needed it. Whenever we reached rock bottom, it happened! Developing intuition was central to my success. I had to tread a path that I had never been on before. In one way it was stressful, in another exhilarating.

In order to finalise matters I filed an application for a legal separation. It would be costly and I had no idea what steps to take. I telephoned the Legal Aid Board to see if I was eligible for assistance. I made an appointment to meet the secretary.

This all seemed effortlessly done and as I made my way up Mount Street to the office my heart sank. I slowly walked up the steps and felt the tidal wave of emotions that I had been avoiding for a long time. Had it come to this? I sat on the steps and sobbed. Were we so low that I had to apply for legal aid? Lonely and bereft

I struggled in the door and walked towards the counter, waiting in line with all the other mortals who were looking equally sad. In my acceptance that this was reality I managed to straighten up. I went through the documents with the secretary. She was very kind and informed me that though it appeared that I qualified for aid on what I had submitted it would need to go through the proper channels. Having no work for the summer and into the autumn months paid off. I was assigned a solicitor and went to see her. She explained the route of separation and how at any time things could change so that we might not even get to court. I said that on my past experience I felt that this would not be my case so I had to prepare myself for the inevitable. I needed to do my homework and make an inventory of expenses and list any income other than what was being received as maintenance. It didn't take long to do this as I had no permanent work. It was an enlightening experience as it made me fully aware of the real cost of bringing up the children. I didn't want to look at it before in case I felt overwhelmed. At times I was feeling selfish demanding maintenance but when I saw the reality it helped clarify just how much we were achieving.

The first of everything after a death or separation is very upsetting. So when it was coming to Annie's first birthday post separation it was all hands on deck. Being the youngest it would be more difficult for her to understand the full extent of the new circumstances especially as all of her friends were being feasted. Roller blades were the in thing and I put a ten-pound deposit on them for her in Champion Sports. The hope was that by the time it came to the birthday extra money would have dropped from the sky. I changed car insurance companies and got a refund just in time for the big day. I wanted with all my heart to bring her to the Fun Factory where she could engage in all the activities, from bouncing castles to slides and free falls. The cost was prohibitive for me but I held firm to the hope that somehow it would be possible. On her actual birthday a letter came in the post from a fellow participant on one of the many courses I attended with the exact amount that was needed. In it were the words "I am so sorry for not writing sooner. I was very grateful for your advice, so much so that I want you to go out and enjoy yourself on this small stipend." Unbelievable!

September brought new developments. Michelle got news of her university options. She phoned me to say she had a place on a science course in The National University of Ireland, Maynooth. I immediately told her to accept it. We will work out the details later. There was no way she could commute such a distance so how were we to manifest this one? I went into the Higher Education Grants office to see if we would be entitled to a grant. There is no doubt but it is better to be born lucky than rich and Michelle always seemed to be able to pull off a hat trick. Thankfully there were no University fees but we had registration and accommodation to think of. She actually qualified for full accommodation and registration fees. The relief in the house was palpable.

If I have a criticism of myself during those years, it would be that I shared too many highs and lows with my children. Some things they did not need to know. Dealing with conflict and silence was exhausting. Sometimes the silence was a reprieve. Part of me wanted them to see how you can survive even in the most difficult of times and also that if you believe strongly enough the Universe in its wisdom will provide for you. It may not be what you want but it will always be what you need. I understood one thing and that is that God will not do one thing for you that you are able to do for yourself. You have to play your part. You have to show up in life and get out there and do something no matter how small. Sitting in front of the television and praying or visualising that something good will come to you without you taking part in your life will not work. I wanted them to understand that. It may not be easy but then my difficult is someone else's easy. I needed to master new ways of being. My easy is also someone else's difficulty. That gave me heart.

Grace needed a boost. She was a great support to me with Annie, reading her stories at bedtime and I wanted to do something for her. Strolling down Dún Laoghaire street, I noticed an offer in a Travel Shop window. A weekend for two in London and it seemed quite reasonable. I spoke to Michelle and she said she would look after Annie and Paul if I should decide to go. "Michelle," I said, "I can only trust that work will come. I am going back down to the travel agent to book it. MasterCard, here I come."

I met the travel agent and explained that I knew nothing about London and have limited sense of direction. I would need to be near the centre, or I might end up permanently lost. He found a good hotel near Oxford Street and felt it would be good for us. I booked the Buddy Holiday Show to make it even better and handed the card. The weekend prior to departure I was giving Michelle a lift to her bus back to the university. There were crowds at the stop and I said that I would take her to the next stop a little further down the way. There was no sign of anyone at the stop and I didn't want to leave her there on her own so we waited in the car for the bus. It sailed past us. This happened again and again. She laughed "Mum, accept the fact, my desire for you to bring me the whole way back is stronger than your desire to put me on a bus." She was right. We then got duly lost on the way as it was not our normal route. "I suppose I will never see the pair of you again when you go to London based on this episode," she grinned.

Late October I was offered four days teaching in a local private Primary school. I would have preferred a state school because they paid more. It was easy money because the children were well behaved. One of the teachers mentioned that there was a job going in Archbishop McQuaid School in Loughlinstown. They were looking for a temporary teacher and she gave me the telephone number.

I telephoned the Principal and he asked if he could interview me the next day. I was praying for this job because it would give me some security knowing that each fortnight a pay cheque would come in the post. I met the Principal that evening. I borrowed my friend's car to go there because mine had given up and was yet again in repair. It was a dreary wet and windy night. He appeared to be very busy and the interview was short and sweet. The only leading question was, "Can you teach Irish?" I told him that I could. "Then the job is yours." I had one stipulation before accepting and that was that I needed to leave early on Friday because I had to catch an evening flight to London. No Problem. Could I observe the class on Thursday so that I could get a feeling for what I was letting myself in for? "One bit of advice for you, don't smile at them until Christmas," he said.

I went in on Thursday as planned. In my hurry to get the job I didn't ask any questions about class size, behavioural difficulties, intellectual difficulties or emotional difficulties. If I had I would have run a mile. I would never have believed that I could have handled this class. Their current teacher was amazingly organised. The walls were filled with examples of their work and they were so quiet you could hear a pin drop. She showed me their test results and it meant absolutely nothing to me. It was a long time since I had examined such things. Fourteen years in the preschool left me out of touch with Micra T and Sigma T tests. I did not have experience with children who could run a business delivering milk or do paper rounds. They were too exhausted to be present, I came in with the idealistic notion that if I was nice to them they would be nice to me. Talk about being naïve!

I arrived on Friday. I made up a few lesson plans thinking that it would be sufficient to keep them occupied for a half a day. Attention span of the majority was limited to five minutes. I now know what a comedian must feel in front of an audience who is not the slightest bit interested in what he has to say, and yet somehow knows that to save his life he must keep them occupied for five and a half hours. This was stand up at its best. What I missed was their ability to sum me up in seconds. I did not have quite the same expertise at summing them up.

Boarding the plane, we were in great spirits. I took a gin and tonic because flying was not my most favourite pastime. Grace was left cold turkey. We landed at Stansted airport, not Heathrow, and I had an initial panic attack until I saw a train that left for Liverpool St. Station. I had planned none of this and had no idea of our itinerary. In my mind we were going to London and we could get a taxi. We got the train and it was dark, wet and scary. We saw the taxis and tentatively asked if we could have one. Green horns let loose.

We got the taxi to the hotel. My stomach lurched. "Grace, are we at the right place?" I asked nervously. There was a man standing outside in top hat and tails. "What if we get out and find that we should be somewhere else and it is already very late?" "Get out," she said. "How?" I asked. "I can't open the door. You open yours." She began to laugh. She couldn't open it either. The taxi man was getting a bit impatient and gave instructions. I had already paid him so he was anxious to get away. Angrily he got out of the taxi in the rain, mouthing some expletives. He went around to Grace's door and opened it. She, pushing the door was not prepared for it to open and nearly fell out. I had tears in my eyes from laughing and she was no better.

We pretended we knew what we were doing and that we were quite used to such surroundings and walked into reception. I handed in my booking form and they handed me the key to the bedroom door. I said thank you and turned to look at Grace and smiled. She walked ahead of me and began to climb the beautiful stairs. We forgot that these places have elevators. "Ma, did you get me the Ritz?" she said in a real Dublin accent. Neither of us had the style to cope with being there. We got into the room and lay on the beds laughing and relieved. The eagles had landed. We were so hungry but we were not going down to that restaurant to mingle among the glamorous guests so we ordered room service for our entire visit. The food minus anxiety was delicious.

Next morning, we showered, had our breakfast and hit the streets. Our first stop was Hamley's toy store. It was pre-Christmas and the whole place was like a winter wonderland. Everything in Hamley's excited us. Our thoughts were with the troops back home. What little gifts could we buy for them? I wanted to get a feel for the city so we strolled around as much as we could. We hadn't the time or money to see the usual sights. We ordered a taxi from the hotel to the West End.

The taxi man was very chatty and told us that there would be no taxi's available after the show because of the Christmas rush. Panic!! "Don't worry," he said, "you are within walking distance or you can get the tube." That was it. Grace said she was not going underground and that was that and anyway I was not familiar with tube stations. She felt claustrophobic in enclosed places. I thought she might relent.

The first half of the show was good but definitely not great. It was interspersed with panic attacks as to how we would get back to the hotel. The second half was much better. I had worried enough in the first half and thought about a plan as to how to get back. I would ask anyone and everyone and focus on getting as far as Piccadilly Circus. I had rehearsed my way back from there. I decided we would go one street at a time. We walked through Covent Garden which, despite my anxiousness was really beautiful. There were many people coming out and I asked again and again until we got to Piccadilly Circus. Phew! Grace's feet were killing her. At that time, I did not show great empathy and stayed quiet. The next morning when I took a look at her cut feet I had compassion and went out to find a Pharmacy. There was nothing open. I thought of a challenge. I had managed plane, train, and walking through London, this time I would love to go on a tube. I went underground for two stops and found a shop open. I got on the tube and went back to the hotel rejoicing that I had managed it. I was pushing me through my own fear factor.

This time together will always be in my memory bank! We never know where life will take us and snatching moments like this is essential. I think of the song Cat's in the Cradle, where in the early years we can be too busy to stop and spend time with our children. Time comes when they grow up and they are too busy or, as in my case, live too far away. We can't turn back the clock.

God will not do one thing for you that you are capable of doing for yourself. You have to play your part. You have to show up in life and get out there and do something no matter how small.

CHAPTER 15

Practising a Different Kind of Teacher

'Hail the irker, for he is your teacher'

Paddy McMahon

W ITH a bottle of Bach flower Rescue remedy to calm the nerves I entered Archbishop McQuaid N.S. on a cold December morning. That first week was a living nightmare. Apart from the behaviours, what really floored me was the organisation of thirty-eight copies in every subject, and doing my best to collect them before they had a chance to deface them. There were at least ten mixed abilities in the classroom. It was 3rd class and most children were about eight years old but some had the behaviours of two year olds, so the slightest remark from a peer emitted a torrent of abuse. Some had specific learning difficulties such as ADHD, dyslexia and dyspraxia which resulted in behavioural difficulties. There was no way one person could meet their needs. They found it extremely difficult to stay on task because what you were asking of them was to conform to a system of education that could not cater for their needs. I planned each day like a military operation and, if for a moment I deviated from the task all hell broke loose. They knew how to distract and caught me off guard regularly. I went home every day shell shocked and exhausted.

If you were to ask what they needed most it would be a secure loving environment with a balance between academic and practical hands on learning, but most of all structure. It would take more than one person in the room to attain this level of interaction. A large percentage were missing any reasonable structure in their lives. They needed to participate in their own learning a lot more than they were doing and since there wasn't enough room in that classroom to organise it in that way, that made it next to impossible. It was crowd control. They found chinks in my armour as I walked into the classroom. I was fair game.

As well as their emotional difficulties I had to deal with my own. I wanted a loving environment where I could teach and yet I had to deal with my own emotional state as I traversed the legal route of separation. I broke down every evening on the way home. I feared going into the classroom and by eleven o' clock the blessed bottle of rescue remedy was nearly finished. What was I to do? I was told, "Don't smile at them until Christmas." Said the Principal P.J. I was beginning to see there was a reason for this. Before I could do anything with the children I had to take a long hard look at me. I had come a great distance in the pre-school. I now had less space and three times the number of children with behavioural difficulties. I began reading books on challenging behaviours. I read all of Tony Humphries books, especially A Different Kind of Teacher. Though it was helpful reading them, putting the ideas into practice was a different matter. I began to see how my ego desperately needed the good opinion of children, teachers and the Principal. It is very easy to write about good practice, another to actually live it.

The study of challenging behaviours and the implications for both teachers and children is relatively new. The heavy hand is no longer acceptable, yet they need to learn to respect authority and the teachers who are doing their best to teach. Many parents came through the old system and based their ideas and opinions of teachers on their own experiences as children. This was a major obstacle because their children were not living their experience, though listening to some parents you would think they were.

I had to come back to Anthony de Mello's work on awareness. When their behaviours pushed me to the wall the question was "Why is this child getting under my skin? What was my biggest fear? I hated being the teacher I hated most, the one who shouts or belittles to gain control. I also hated being the naïve fool falling prey to their manipulations. Who was feeling this pain the most? It was me. They rolled out of the classroom pushing and shoving and in high spirits. Why was I having so much difficulty gaining control? I hated in any way being harsh and yet I needed to be one hundred per cent clear that they could not shout across the classroom, throw rubbers, rulers, call each other mongos or slappers. They could not shout profanities or sneer at children who did not have a stable home environment or at a child who had specific learning difficulties. They could not walk up the classroom knocking a child's books off the table, especially a child whom they knew would be deeply affected. They could not threaten me with being sued if by any chance I tripped over their bags and fell against them. They could not scribble on desks or run towards the door knocking any child in sight to be the first out. They could not grab everything in sight because they wanted it and most of all there could be no throwing of chairs or punching other children. So how was I to turn all these could not's into positives!

I did not want to hurt any child as some had enough hurt in their lives. They had a happy knack of bringing me into their familiar territory. I would end up shouting at them and then they were off the hook. Look, it is teacher's fault because see she is the one doing me harm and not the other way around. They had the knack to slide out of responsibility for their behaviour. It wasn't always easy to see who did what to whom and who began the fracas. Though I would begin with the right intention of solving the problem I never quite knew how they managed to turn it around to my being the one out of kilter. They were professionals at this. They were doing exactly what I had experienced before. Semantics at play! Some were used to being shouted at so this was not a problem for them. My problem was my need to be kind and loving at all times according to my belief on what kind and loving meant. I did not see that sometimes you need to be quite tough to love! You need to develop positive leadership skills. They needed a moral compass. This is why for the first six weeks it was hell. I wanted to be firm but kind and they tried their best to bring me back to losing my temper. They knew how to handle a fractious situation but not loving kindness from a teacher. It didn't always work for me but neither did it always work for them to provoke me into someone they were used to.

Once I was able to see my own vulnerability I was in a position to choose a different response minus the emotional outburst. Their control over me diminished by degrees and, as it did, my need to over control them ceased. I knew that if they began to move up an octave I was assured I had the capability to bring them down an octave and back into balance. A lower tone of voice has more chance of being heard. Every day I fell in through my home front door and fell into the nearest armchair. What didn't help at the time was dealing with my own children's complaints about teachers. I changed my mind about teachers, they were all saints in my head. There is no doubt that my own children had their difficulties but at that time I was just about keeping my head above water. I had three weeks to go before Christmas and then I could use the time to recoup my energies.

God Bless the author Janet Sahaffi. She gave me an insight into how to deal with difficulties especially if you are someone who can be easily swayed into thinking that you are the person at fault. I could witness a pupil stick a pencil into another pupil while at the same time, he would completely deny that he even had a pencil in his hand. He would then project blame onto the innocent victim beside him and begin a slanging match unequalled in my experience. Before you knew where you were, there was total uproar as others joined in the fray to either support the perpetrator or the victim. "Miss he wasn't even near the mongo." What would immediately come to mind is that you wanted peace at all costs so you took the usual route of silencing all. The victim ended up extremely resentful and later in the day would be the one to start up another episode.

As I was doing my best to keep order and trying to teach, the victim concentrated on revenge. If I clearly saw the incident, then I was on to a winner. I never got caught up in their shenanigans again. The rule is clear, hands and feet to yourself. "I never touched him Miss," was met with, "I saw you." No matter how they tried to convince me otherwise I repeated the mantra and clearly stated the consequences. I stuck by that. Minor demeanours had minor consequences. The one thing the boys loved was football and if I was to have any impact I had to hit them where it hurt. "You stay with me during little break. No football this morning for you." It was my only weapon. I found that written work was the main problem. Many did not have the skills to put their ideas on paper. Vocabulary was limited. Some did not know the value of their thoughts and undermined themselves.

This surely came to me strongly when I discovered that I had one boy Liam who had infinite knowledge about the habits of turtles. He reminded me of the boy in the film Kes. It was a story about a young boy and his kestrel in the North of England. Liam had severe dyslexia and found it very difficult to read or write. Yet when he spoke about animals he became animated. I see him clearly at the back of the class as he stood up to talk about turtles. I could have listened to him for hours. Once he went into the zone of speaking there was no impediment. I wish now I had the insight to have taken him out of the classroom and taped his conversations. What I realised was, that when you took the time to find out what interested them, you were able to harness that interest and use it to teach reading, writing and arithmetic. Addition and subtraction related to milk and paper rounds achieved a lot. Reading in relation to football contracts! What did I want from them? I wanted them to have literacy and mathematical skills. Geography and history could always come later once they had basic mastery.

If I could tailor the curriculum around their interest, then I could manage to get them on board for subjects they had difficulty with. Mathematics was the biggest problem, not the basic mathematical skills but problem solving. Problem solving in any area of their lives was a difficulty. They would react to what was in front of them dramatically and decisively. You would be called either a wanker or a mongo and that covered everything. I found that if I taught them how to solve relationship problems they were also accessible to solving mathematical problems. What it was doing was getting them to slow down to see, see what the bigger picture was asking of them. They loved music but if I introduced a song that was of no interest to them, I was told immediately what they thought of it.

I envied my neighbouring teacher who appeared to have such control that her pupils would do exactly what she wanted. She had been teaching this age group for some years and was extremely helpful to me. She had work sheets garnered together over many years and if ever I was not succeeding in getting a concept in mathematics across to them, I would ask for her help. I would look at her art work so professionally presented on the wall outside her door and it would send me into a depression. Then I would look at my exhibits and see that each one was uniquely theirs and it would give me heart. I was doing my best to uncover the individuality of the children while at the same time keep some sort of order. I began to see just how capable they were. Once I had order then I had some chance in seeing individual needs. I made it to the end of the year.

I needed a rest. I went to the west of Ireland to a Health Farm for five days. This was the funniest five days' holiday I ever spent. We were like the girls of St. Trinian's. The lady who owned the operation did not appear to be interested in either us or the centre. For breakfast, we got three pieces of fruit on a plate. My mother-in-law would have had one description for the apples and it would be "mausey." You did not need to be an interpreter to understand that the apples had long gone past their sell by date. We were allowed hot water and honey for energy before exercise. Whether you were eight or eighty you got the same treatment and the same exercises. Two elderly German ladies were expected to jump around like us. Lunch was soup with some salad and brown bread. Dinner was mausey fruit again. The afternoons were for walks except for Wednesday where it was advertised that we could do as we pleased.

At breakfast time the lady approached our table. "Who came by car?" A few of us put up our hands. "That is fine. Can you bring the ladies who do not have cars with you for the afternoon?" I was fuming. I wanted to be as far away from responsibility as I could and being made responsible on my one afternoon off annoyed me. It was the manipulative way she asked that got me. I said nothing until the following morning.

It came to a moment when I felt it would be convenient to say how I felt. I practised this exercise. I wanted to do this on my own and it wasn't easy to find a quiet moment but it came. I spoke quite clearly about how I felt at having to take someone with me at a time when I wanted peace and quiet. The brochure indicated that transport would be available for anyone who came on buses or trains, I did not think that that transport would be the rest of us. She was responsible for the group and I did not want this to happen again during my time there. She stormed out. Speaking out was my lesson. She could deal with hers. We were good for each other and though the place left a lot to be desired we laughed, cried, detoxed, lost weight and got plenty of fresh air. I, who had been off coffee for two years, went into Ennis and ordered a large coffee and so began my love affair all over again. What more did we want?

I got home and saw my pay slip. Happy days! I opened it to see I had little or no pay. I phoned the Department of Education frantically. I had begun my employment in December and I would not be entitled to pay for the summer months. I told them I was returning to school in September as my contract was signed. This made no difference. I asked if they could at least send me some documentation to say that they would give me a rebate in September as soon as I returned to school. I needed that for the bank. Thankfully with this document I was able to secure finance for the summer.

I had advance warning of my next year. In a dream I could see two boys who were to be challenging. The dream was clear. The Principal had them pinned to the floor. I knew when I woke up that I was being warned of the difficulties ahead. The first day back at school I saw the children in the hall. Without having to be told who they were I could see them acting out in a manner they were accustomed to. They were exactly how they appeared in the dream, so it wasn't difficult to spot them. On the way to the classroom they managed to punch any child who happened to be in their way. School rules or classroom rules meant nothing to them. Danny, the main culprit, talked out of turn incessantly.

One morning it got too much for me and I walked towards him. I put him at the back because at the front he had an audience. He entertained non-stop throughout the day. As I walked towards him I noticed that he flinched. He looked at me with his huge brown eyes and leaned backwards in his chair, his eyes full of fear. I asked him to be quiet and if he could just stay silent for five minutes it would help my poor head. I even told him that I would let him know when the five minutes were up. I needed space to gather my thoughts and his silence would help. He said nothing. The moment silence hit the room the other boy Jimmy started interrupting. Danny, seeing this shouted, "Would ye shut up ye mongo, did you not hear what miss said, yer doin her head in."

The moment the words came out of his mouth all hell broke loose. It was worse than I could have imagined it, yet I felt so touched that Danny should defend my honour. Some way or other he had made a way into my heart. Trust was beginning to enter our relationship. No matter how I tried to protect him from himself I seemed to be making little headway. I tried time and time again to defend him but he didn't make it easy for people. Constantly being argumentative didn't help his cause. Once he got an idea in his head he would stick with it and continue to argue his case until you relented. The thing was that what he would say would have an element of truth in it but it might be too close to the bone for another to accept his findings. This style of relating continued for the entire year, yet in the mayhem of it all we did get some work done.

Each day I felt this undercurrent of stress in my stomach. Why? When the children were disruptive the stress escalated. Again, why? What were my expectations of them and more importantly what were my expectations of myself? What were the prevailing thoughts in my head when the stress reached its peak? Reflecting on this in the quiet of my own home I realised it wasn't the actual disruption but the fear of what my colleagues might think of me. Would the Principal think I was extremely inefficient especially as I was next door to the most efficient? Silence prevailed in that room always. The comparisons and permanently equating my efforts with the efforts of another, were the root cause of my stress. I did not measure up to a standard in my mind.

Once I saw that, the fear and stress began to subside. I was afraid of what P.J the Principal would think about my efforts to keep control over certain children who were next to impossible to engage in the learning process. I was not asking for help. That was the beginning of the release. I could also see that I was using a different approach and was actually getting results.

I had to do my diploma. P.J thinking kindly on my behalf asked if I would put Danny and Jimmy into another classroom for the day. I said that was pointless because Inspectors never get an opportunity to see these guys in action. His response was that you have other days to show him and perhaps it was a bit risky on diploma day.

We went along nicely until mathematics. Danny was having difficulty and seeing that he was a bit challenging, the Inspector decided to be the Good Samaritan. He was trying to help Danny to which Danny replied, "That is not what Miss said." The Inspector tried to show him the error of his ways but he continued to get the same response. "Miss didn't say dat." I went down to see what was happening and showed him where he was getting stuck. The Inspector seeing this ran over to see what I did and declared, "That is exactly what I was telling you." "Ye didn't say dat, Miss said it." The Inspector reached a high level of frustration. Danny continued to talk out of turn and it wasn't helped by his friend Jimmy hitting his table like a buck rabbit. The Inspector said that if he was the teacher he would keep these two boys in after school until 4 pm every day until they learned how to behave. Hearing this Jimmy placed his eraser on to the end of his ruler and shot it right into the Inspector's face. Leaving the room, he said, "I am glad it is you and not me coming in here tomorrow."

Sadly, Danny died an accidental death aged fifteen. At that time, I had resigned from teaching and had not heard of his death until the funeral was over. I had been given a gift of tickets to listen to Frances Black singing in the National Concert hall two days after his funeral. I knew that Danny had not been able to cope in Secondary School and I was doing my best to accept his death. Little platitudes like "Perhaps he is in a much better place" and many more sayings like it, didn't help but I managed to put the pain aside momentarily. Frances in her usual style captured the hearts of the audience and then began to sing, "It's just a wall of tears I've got to get over." I began to cry inconsolably and couldn't stop. I loved that child. Three weeks before he died, as I was driving by, I had seen him on his bicycle. I beeped the horn at him. He got down off the bike and seemed confused, then seeing me he frantically waved his arm. I could see him through my rear view mirror. His last goodbye!

I became aware that I was seeing the children through my pain. One young boy was particularly difficult. He would love to torment his classmates and start a row. I could not deny he was provocative?

One day I was out sick and a young teacher came in as a substitute. Seemingly, on yard duty he was particularly difficult and had upset her. The following day I came back and heard the story. I went to P.J and asked could he be removed from the class and corrected. I saw the child lower his head and read that as shame. This really upset me so much that it opened up a can of worms in me. What I was actually seeing was me, the small child, not this young fellow. He marched back to class as if nothing had happened and was seen as a hero. I reacted to that situation through the memory and experience of my childhood. It triggered a memory. I responded to that memory as if a knife had pierced my heart.

You don't need to go back to the people who hurt you in the past to understand that the present people who trigger you are reminders of that past. See this and learn from it. I understood that when my emotions were in flux was not the time to deal with a situation. If I had a difficulty with P.J I usually waited for a few days for that energy to die down. Then I would tackle the problem.

He said later "Liz, I hated when you came to me and asked for ten minutes of my time. I knew I was going to be challenged in the politest manner!" I let him know how I felt about a situation and then left him to act or not act. What was important for me was to speak out. He did not know that he was my guinea pig. I knew he would listen to me, and would not hold a grudge. That is why I felt comfortable telling him how I felt. I practiced the development of my awareness skills on him, knowing it was safe to do so. I also clarified that I was not demanding he act on any situation, how he responded to what I said was up to him as Principal.

I came to see that feminine energy is extremely important. The feminine side is the nurturer and the intuitive side. My understanding of the feminine was that of being a second class citizen. Her challenge is to act on her intuitiveness. To do that women need to access their masculine side. For men, their challenge is to access intuitiveness to complete their masculine side. No blame! I grew up with the idea that behind every great man there was a woman. I wasn't happy to stay in the shadow but had difficulty coming out of it.

In 1998 I accidently formed a garden in the school for children who were experiencing behavioural difficulties. There was a student teacher in on teaching practice and his Inspector had come to observe him. I wanted to get Danny out so that he had some chance of success so I said to the Inspector that we were going out to plant seeds. The children loved the development of the garden. We entered a competition and when the adjudicators came to the school to look at their efforts they said that anyone who managed to rustle up such enthusiasm deserved a prize and we had to go to the local Town Hall to collect it. The prize gave me enough money to continue on.

The following year I was moved to Learning Support. It gave me space to include children throughout the school. One day I noticed an odd looking figure pass my window on a bicycle. He looked like a caricature of Orville Wright on his first mission, complete with goggles. Immediately a judgement crossed my mind based on his appearance. I went up to him and introduced myself. He told me he was working on a local project and was asked to come over and see if I needed help. I asked him if he knew anything about plants and flowers. He assured me that he was the man. He also said that he had grown up in one of those awful institutions and wanted to give something back to children. He didn't want them to have his experience of education. His name was Joe. We worked together for months.

I noticed his simple but effective way of disciplining the children. To one child he said, "Go back down and wash yer mouth out, I won't have ye cursin' up here." The child's usual response was to lose the head and completely deny he had done anything. This time it was different. I asked him. "What do you need to do before going back up to Joe." "Wash me mouth out", he replied. "Then away you go and apologise." He walked back up the hill slowly, stood contrite in front of Joe and said "Sorry, Joe." This was nothing short of a miracle. "Right, you understand, no more of that mouthin." "Yeah." "Then, get your shovel." The behaviour was corrected, the relationship remained intact. Liz," he said, "Those kids need your skill, not your pity." I never forgot that. I learned more from Joe on how to work with children in a disadvantaged area than from any lecturer in College.

These children helped me become the teacher I longed to become. A different kind of teacher. Without their input my ideas would have stayed with my feet firmly planted in the clouds. Ideology is of little use to you as you are floundering on the ground, if you are not prepared to see how it can be brought into practice. They helped me take the ideals out of my head and bring at least some of them to earth.

The people who initially upset you should not be in a position of control over you for the rest of your life. Unless you look at this they will have this power in your present day relationships. Where they become alive in your life is when you come in contact with personalities who are mirrors of those early relationships. In front of them you become the child and respond accordingly.

I looked closely at their body language and said to the solicitor, 'There is little difference between what they are doing down there and what the horse traders are doing over in Smithfield'

CHAPTER 16

Free Legal Aid

'They cannot take away our self-respect if we do not give it to them'
Mahatma Gandhi

I LEFT the work of the marital separation to the professionals. I answered letters sent to me from the opposite side as soon as they came in just to get it moving quickly. They sent letters to the opposition and they got stuck in time. When enough details were prepared I was given the name of my Barrister. She was a tough lady who I felt knew her job. She looked at the figures in front of her and said that this was pretty straightforward. I was very confident in her ability to get a fair hearing.

I didn't see her again until two weeks before the court case. She asked to meet me for a final look over some details. I met her in the yard of the Law Library and we walked towards her room. I said as we strolled, that what I wanted most was right of residence in the family home for me and the children because my husband was now resident in his mother's house as she was in a nursing home. She got extremely angry. "Don't you tell me my job," she shouted. "I will tell you what you are entitled to." She could have hit me with a sledge hammer. I looked over to my solicitor who put her head down and didn't make eye contact.

We went into her room and she sat down noisily. She was in some humour. I have no idea what I ignited in her but it was something powerful. Was I not victim enough for her? Was she in this business to massage her ego by taking on cases pro bono? Did we poor unfortunates have to accept everything on her terms even though it is our livelihoods that are at stake? Where is truth and justice in this system? Should I have gone cap in hand to her? Does being at the mercy of the State mean you have no voice or no entitlements other than what this lady declares? I sat there in shock and waited for what she had to offer. "Why should his assets be tied up because of you? Why should he have to wait until you decide to grow up? You have a trade and you can take it where you like. My advice to you is to go out and look for alternative accommodation in Stillorgan for you and the children, or you could take yourself to the country if that is not a possibility. There is nothing keeping you here."

I said I was trying to minimize the possible damage to my children especially the youngest who was only ten years old. "Pierce the boil and get on with it," she said. I sobbed in front of her. "You," she said, "have not moved on. You are still stuck. Get over your emotions." I did my best to walk out with dignity though I wished the ground would open up and swallow me. I struggled across the road to the nearest pub to buy a cup of coffee because I was in no fit state to drive the car. "If this is who I have representing me then I am finished," I thought. What planet did that lady inhabit? The case was set for Friday morning. I had made arrangements for a day off school. At 6.30 on Thursday evening the solicitor phoned to say the case was cancelled. John did not give in his P60 form – a statement of earnings on time. Something as simple as that had derailed it. A new date was set for July.

I bided my time for a few days and picked up the phone to the solicitor. I told her I was not happy with my barrister. Anyone who felt free to treat a client in this way could not be working for my best interests. "I want a new barrister, someone who can hear me out and someone who will listen to me." She told me that I couldn't do that as this lady had put in an enormous amount of work. "That may be so," I told her, "but she is not working for us, she has her own agenda."

Two days later I got a call to say I had a new Barrister. I went to meet him and the first thing he said to me was that automatically the children deserved the right to live in the family home as there was no reason to disrupt them. What is more, he said, he would work on the right to remain there until the youngest child was 23. Now the Gods were with me!

July 23rd 1998 arrived. I didn't want to look the poor relation so I went out and bought myself some new clothes. I trusted this barrister and I was also given a new solicitor. Previously I had two women now it was two men. I went into the Riverbank Courthouse and waited anxiously. When I met the barrister he said for some reason we were not listed for that day though both sides were present. He knew that there was some human error somewhere so he told me he was going to grovel with the Judge. We were told that we were to wait and listen for our names to be called. A bell would ring from time to time and names would be called. By the time our names came up the Judge expected most of the work to be done. Both barristers moved outside. I could see them haggling under the canopy of the bus stop. I looked closely at their body language and said to the solicitor, "There is little difference between what they are doing down there and what the horse traders are doing over in Smithfield." "Clarify," he said. "Think of it this way. The horse traders are looking for the best deal financially and those two guys are doing exactly the same. Similar skills, different employment." "Are you a mystic or what?" he asked. "No, just an observer of human beings," I replied.

They came back up to find that our names had been called but not one of us heard them. Again the Barrister said he would have to do even more serious grovelling. The Judge made the stipulation that she would hear us out but only if the documents were almost ready for signing. Finally, we all heard the call and I went into the courtroom. I felt in a surreal frame of mind. It was as if I had done everything I could do and now it was in the lap of the Gods. I did not have to take the stand to defend myself. I had nothing to fear. I had prayed constantly to be shown what was fair, that we get not one penny more or a penny less than what we were entitled to and that is exactly what happened. Thanks to the Barrister who challenged me to find a voice and the Barrister who could hear me. Both were significant players! I walked out the door in freedom imagining that I would not have to do this again!

Sometimes people do things for you so that they won't have to have a bad feeling. They call it charity and you are expected to be grateful.

CHAPTER 17

Time to Breathe

'Go tie your camel to the post. God will not do one thing for you that you are capable of doing for yourself'

Anon

THOUGH I was delighted that this part of our lives was complete I was drained of all feeling and emotion. I needed some time to breathe and strolled up to Adam and Eve's church to sit and give thanks but also to digest what had happened. There is an indescribable void when the dust settles. A shattering of dreams and illusions! Grief for what could have been!

What could I do for the two youngest to take their minds off the heaviness of the preceding days? I booked a bed and breakfast in Middleton Co. Cork and decided to take them on four days' holidays. They had never stayed in such accommodation so it was all new for them. I had discovered that I was paid eight hundred pounds extra, something I hadn't been expecting. It was a rebate of hard earned yard duty money. In those days, one teacher, a whistle and three hundred pupils let loose. We set off in the car hoping it was fit enough to survive the journey. We were in high spirits. Paul mimicking Mr. Byrne's song "See my vest" from the Simpsons made us laugh. It took us longer than expected to get to Middleton so when we actually arrived at our destination we were more than pleasantly surprised. We hadn't expected a kettle in the room or biscuits and the first thing we did was to make ourselves tea and coffee. We sat on the floor munching biscuits, planning our trip and absorbing the atmosphere. We were cocooned in an orb of contentment.

I was determined that these few days would be totally about them and the following day we set off for Trabolgan. This is a fantastic place for kids with every amenity geared towards them. They spent a long time in the pool enjoying the wave machine. Paul even met one of his friends from Dublin. We did as much as we could in those short hours and enjoyed every moment. We worked our way towards Cork city hoping to find directions to Dingle easily enough. No sat navigators then. Every part of that time seemed to be synchronised. I had no idea how to get from Cork to Dingle but as we made our way Paul noticed a sign for Blarney Castle. "Mum, we have to go there to kiss the Blarney Stone." It is meant to give you the gift of the gab - "conversation." As if Paul ever needed assistance in communication! We had to walk a winding stairway to get to the top. When we reached there it became clear what was expected of us. We had to lie on our backs and lean forward to kiss this stone. This old man held us to protect us from a fall from the top of the castle. It was quite precarious.

The problem was how to get out of Blarney. There was a cycle race and road blocks everywhere. A policeman told us we could find a way to Dingle if we went through the hills. We followed the direction of his finger and continued for some miles. There in the middle of nowhere was a shop named The de Mello Emporium. We had to stop and investigate. The girl at the counter explained that the owner was interested in some Indian fella called de Mello and he called the place after him. There is no such thing as coincidence! Why did I get guided there?

My book Awareness always came with me. Whenever I felt the need to keep on track to observe what difficulty I was going through, I would take out that book and pick a page. Was this a sign that I was to continue with Awareness? Unusual to say the least! We dined in the Emporium, nothing more than sandwiches and drinks, content to be on our way.

We got to Dingle late afternoon and set about looking for accommodation. We found a place on the Connor Pass road that was comfortable. Once established we headed into the town for something to eat and later strolled around the area investigating what we would do the following day. Fungi the dolphin was high on our list. We had to see him. We booked our tickets though Annie was apprehensive about any boat trip. We set off on the trip and moved out into the bay. No sign of Fungi anywhere. The boatmen knew exactly how to attract him and there was this play that goes on that both they and Fungi understood. He emerged from the water. The surprise of everyone on board rocked it and it tilted to one side. Even Annie who was afraid of boats ran across to the other side to get a sighting. Whatever it is about this animal even the most sceptical are enthralled! The power of a present moment experience! We rarely remember the day dreaming, the useless thoughts, but significant present moment awareness stays alive forever. Reluctantly we made our way to the shore and as it was Paul's birthday we headed to the nearest Italian restaurant for a celebratory lunch. The restaurant did not disappoint as the two waitresses were Italian and sang, "Happy birthday, dear blonde boy," to him. The grin from ear to ear was worth a photograph. He had recently died his hair blonde. From there we attempted a tour of the peninsula. We managed to get to the top of Connor Pass and joined the hikers who scrambled across the rocks to the lake that was hiding behind them. I sat there by the lake for some time contemplating while they climbed nearby. Peace at last!

Our four days were coming to an end and none of us wished to return quite yet. It wasn't just the activities but the lack of tension and the pleasant companionship. Nothing was allowed spoil this trip. On the way home we visited Crag Caves. This was unexpectedly beautiful. The music as we moved through the stalactites and stalagmites set the scene. The lighting gave it a mystical appearance. One last thing I had to do for Paul. The car park was empty and I gave him his first driving lesson. It was a lovely ending to a magnificent few days. When we got back I knew that I had to find a way to let go the travesties of the previous four years. I had never been on a sunshine holiday ever. Grace would be joining Michelle in University that autumn so if I was to go away it had to be before we all returned to school.

Shirley Valentine did it so why not I? Corfu was the destination of choice! The excitement of booking the ticket was soon replaced by apprehension leaving the brood behind. What if something happened while I was away, what if the plane crashed? I couldn't afford a taxi and there were no Air Coaches then. I didn't want to have to say goodbye to the children at the airport but due to circumstances beyond my control it happened that Paul and Annie were with me. Marie my lovely old friend came with us. Annie was clinging to me like a leech and as the time to go through the departure gates beckoned she, sensing this, wrapped her gangly legs around my waist. She noticed something from her exalted position and asked me for some coins. I didn't know what she needed them for, until I saw her sitting on the steps counting. She was so engrossed in this activity that her little head was turned sideways obviously calculating her purchase. I saw her go over to the shop assistant who helped her count out exactly what was needed. She came back to me running asking me to take this little Leprechaun with me to keep me safe. I wrapped her and Finnegan the Leprechaun up in my arms as I tearfully said goodbye, promising to be back in one week's time. I invested in my children. I didn't realise how much I depended on them for my emotional survival. I had to do something for me and this holiday was a new beginning. While the plane made its way down the runway I allowed myself the luxury of being excited. There was no turning back. I was off. The trip was a very good experience because it showed me that going anywhere on your own is possible. Not being with someone meant that I was free to come and go as I pleased. I was also able to meet many people that perhaps would never have approached me if I were with a companion. A new departure in engaging with life. Observing the boundaries I created and the ones that were created for me, I made a promise to myself to move through them as they presented themselves.

I returned to school in September and by October life went into overdrive. Grace also got a place in The National University of Ireland, Maynooth and we needed to sort out her accommodation. This time we were not entitled to a full grant due to my permanent employment. The girls needed to commute a long distance each day. This was exhausting for us all. The bus service to the train station was intermittent so I had to wake them at 6am each morning to get them to the station and come home to get the others up out of bed for school. It was like I had done a day's work prior to going to work.

My sister suggested that during my mid-term break we meet in some European city for a weekend. I chose Paris as it was one on my list of cities to experience. I had lost a lot of weight but that was understandable considering the gruelling schedule. I wanted to make the most of a few days' rest. We took one of the sightseeing city buses. With limited time it was also a wonderful way to find out what would be worth exploring later. She was intent on going to a show and I left her to speak to the lady at the counter. In the middle of the conversation I overheard her say the Folies Bergere. With that I ran to her and said we must do this. She looked at me quizzically. Believe me when I explain you will understand. "What was that all about?" she asked. I asked if she could remember a time when our other sister wanted to go to France as an au pair. Dad was refusing to sign the passport form declaring she would end up on the dance floor in the Folies Bergere. He eventually signed it under duress.

We dressed up for the show, a cabaret of sixties music and enjoyed it immensely. At the very end the cast ran into the audience and pulled out the nearest members. The first to be pulled up on to the stage were the two of us. We were flabbergasted! Looking heavenwards I said, "Ok Dad, we get the point, finally your worst nightmare came true!"

I returned home and I continued to lose weight. I was exhausted permanently. The girls were also exhausted so I asked them to go to the doctor. They had a virus so I thought perhaps I too should get checked out. I was hanging in there for the Christmas school holidays. I needed rest. The permanent thirst was also concerning. Nothing could quench it. After school on 23rd December I, too, made an appointment with my doctor. When I spoke of my schedule he said not to worry about the tiredness, but to take time out during the holidays. "A schedule like what you're experiencing would make any mere mortal exhausted" I then mentioned the thirst. He checked sugar levels. They were sky high. He looked at me gravely and said that my next stop would be the local hospital. I had diabetes. I nearly keeled over with fright. I went home. It was dark, miserable and raining. We didn't have mobile phones so I couldn't contact the girls. I put my key in the door and made straight for the kettle. Not understanding fully, the nature of diabetes I made a slice of toast with jam. I needed someone to mind the children. Annie was only ten. I couldn't leave her until I could get someone to mind her. No one was around, my near neighbours were all busy with Christmas. I waited until one of them returned and explained the situation. I couldn't get through to John. I drove down to the hospital, parked the car and walked into casualty. I was lying on a trolley when my elderly friend Marie Donegan arrived. Neither of us could speak. The nurse came around and checked my levels again. Needless to say after the toast it was even higher. Later, I was brought to a ward. The girls were shopping so when they returned to a dark house they had no idea what was happening.

What happened to me? I had a full medical in September and that also included a check for sugar levels and there was no sign of diabetes. How was I going to afford this? What was going to happen to my job? When I was told that diabetics have free medication I breathed a sigh of relief. Next question was how was this going to affect my work? I needed to be able to work? We all depended on it.

Being Christmas most patients were sent home so it was just a few of us in the ward. I wanted to sleep to help the nightmare disappear. The girl next to me was playing with a Furbie doll that made this horrendous sound. After what seemed like hours of this I asked her to turn it off. When the doctor came in he could see I was agitated. He told me there were worse things in life than diabetes. I told him that in mine at that very moment, it was the worst thing, but that in time I would come to terms with it. "Right now, I have four children that still need me to be healthy and I feel the pressure of it" He got the message, and from then on he was extremely kind to me. I felt that I needed more than awareness. I phoned a friend who told me that I needed to go and examine my life. That if I had attracted diabetes then there was something I was doing wrong. I definitely needed to examine my life but to be told that at this time was cruel. I did not feel that I was totally responsible for this. People who are experiencing illnesses do not need a dose of guilt added to their already burgeoning woes.

I had never missed a Christmas Eve. It was definitely a lesson in life goes on whether you are there or not. The girls got a Santa suit from a friend. It was an awful eighties affair but in the dark it would do. Paul was commandeered to wear this and to make his journey across the garden at an unearthly time of the morning. They timed it well. Tracks were made earlier by pulling the trampoline across and leaving the remains of shredded carrot on the ground as a sign of Rudolph's presence. The timing was perfect. Grace went to Annie and told her that Santa was crossing the garden and he had a huge, black sack on his back. They ducked down low beneath the window in case Santa saw them. Grace could see Paul making his way slowly and prayed he would hurry up a bit in case Annie would recognise him. The excitement was worth it all. She ran back down to her bed and Grace tucked her in. She told her not to worry because more than likely Santa would leave all the presents in the sitting room but she must sleep. I was allowed out from the hospital for a few hours on Christmas day. It soon became clear to the medics that I needed insulin injections so I had to have training in how to inject. They reassured me that in time it would not be the injecting that would be the problem but the diet. I had never a sweet tooth prior to this so I didn't see it as a problem. What I didn't understand was that all carbohydrate would be glucose forming and all fruits have fructose.

When I got home the girls were exhausted. They declared that they had no idea how I functioned with so little sleep each Christmas. What I realised was that one way or another everything would be fine in the end.

The hypos were terrifying. The feeling that perhaps this time the sugar would not rise was what scared me most. The tingling sensation in the mouth, the thumping heart and the sense that I was going down a deep tunnel into unconsciousness, that feeling of non-space, not having any idea where I was in relation to the space around me, was frightening. As I lay down praying the sugars would come back up it took its time. Getting a hypo at home is frightening enough; suddenly getting one in a car park is on a different level. Your whole sense of direction gets lost. You have no idea where you are or how to get where you need to go. It is not a disease you can take for granted, though when you do acclimatise to it, you can manage it well.

It was a month before I could return to school. By then I was confident I could deal with it. What helped also were two children in the classroom who also suffered and who also needed to inject. Even though I had to deal with their difficulties since September, I still did not fully understand the implications.

They were quite familiar with what they had to do and were very independent. It was surely a learning curve.

The greeting I received in the corridor from a young pupil made my day. "Miss I couldn't have stuck another day without you here, and I am tellin' the god's honest truth." For Annie and Paul, they lived with the reality of diabetes each day. When I needed help they gave it, when I got a hypo they waited with me. The stress of this deeply affected Annie. It all got too much. The separation, the two houses and my illness shocked her system. As soon as I had found a way to manage the disease, she broke down. "Mum, I want to go home," she said. "You are home." "No," she cried, "This is not home, home is with God and I want to go back." I reassured her she was safe with me, that I would always be there for her. I didn't feel that confident but did my utmost to help her feel its truth. I rocked her back and forth, holding her tightly, comforting her and prayed for help.

She was having a dreadful time in school. Her beautiful teacher was out on maternity leave. With stress, her short term memory for facts was affected. She found homework difficult. She, who was one of the best at mathematics in her class, could not do them. I made an appointment to meet her new teacher. As I entered the room I was met by an icy breeze. This frosty lady stood straight in front of me. I explained the situation and asked for some leniency as we moved through this time. If I had spoken to the wall, I would have received more empathy. The hounding continued. It was now a mortal sin not to do homework. When I heard this I knew Annie could not have made this up. This was something I would have heard in my childhood but mortal and venial sins were no longer used. The memory of what I had to deal with on my own with a similar teacher in my childhood came flooding back. This time I made an appointment to meet the Principal. She was not in any way supportive. She wasn't going to listen. "What we have here is a fine young teacher. She is excellent at her job." I didn't believe her for a moment, based on my personal experience of my meeting with her.

There was no obvious solution. I telephoned the Psychologist Dr Tony Humphries who happened to have been a facilitator on many of the courses I attended and outlined what was happening. He said "based on what you are saying and, if what you are saying is true, what we have here is a case of emotional abuse." I was not one for molly coddling my children any more, and they were well familiar with my telling them to keep their heads down if what was going on did not concern them. Only in cases where I knew they did not have the skills to deal with it, did I take action. I telephoned the school and spoke with the Principal. She was taken aback at the Psychologist's viewpoint. She telephoned my school a few days later and asked if I would be prepared to take Annie out of school for two weeks. Her usual teacher would be back after Easter. I stipulated that this was not something I would encourage.

"For one, you are the Principal and you are responsible for the well-being of the children. If I take Annie out, then I am saying to her that she can run away from the challenges in life and I am also indirectly telling her that she cannot trust the adults who are meant to be her teachers. This I will not do. You too, will not be taking responsibility. I expect that you will sort out this problem and make it known to this teacher that she discontinues her relentless demand that Annie complies with her demands as they are out of order right now. She hasn't the health to do this. She can make up for it later, but right now she needs to feel safe in life"

She mentioned that the cause of stress was due to family circumstances. My blood boiled. I agreed that this was a major part of the problem but it did not need to be made worse by the behaviour of a teacher. I asked her to put her request that Annie stay out of school for two weeks in writing. Needless to say it never happened. I was being pushed time and again to find that voice, to search for truth within and without. I had no intention of giving this teacher a difficult time but she, too, had to take responsibility for her own insecurities but not at the expense of my child. After Easter her loving teacher returned and all became well with the world for a while. In the past every cell in my body would have been terrified dealing with the Principal. What I was witnessing was the practical application of awareness and a knowing that truth is like an arrow. When you keep within the orbit of truth in these situations then the outcome has a better chance of being positive.

None of us are exempt from the swings and arrows of life but that does not give us the right to dump our anger and insecurities on others. Time after time it is because we are unaware of what we are doing.

For the party that is being challenged this altercation gives them an opportunity to stand up and be counted. Life will always give us the lessons we need to become whole.

CHAPTER 18

Chrysalis
Holistic Centre

'Holding on to resentment is like holding on
to a burning coal. You are the one to suffer'

Anon

EACH year Chrysalis Centre in Co. Wicklow sent me their six monthly programme. I had attended some courses that were extremely helpful to me in the past and it was a place of refuge for me when my energy levels were down. As I scanned the contents to see what was available I noticed that a Jesuit from India was coming from the Anthony de Mello Centre. He was giving a seven day retreat the following July. I looked at his name Dr P. J. Francis and thought that if he was half as good as Patrick Francis, author of The Grand Design and my spiritual mentor in 1994, it would be worth attending. I took a chance on sending a deposit.

Michelle and Grace took charge of the family so that I could go. They were in good hands. They had plenty of experience babysitting and had developed skills in dealing with challenging situations. They set up a system whereby each one had their responsibilities. No one escaped the chart. I had full confidence that all would be well. The day for departure arrived. My car was in being serviced and was not ready on time. I telephoned Clare in Chrysalis to let her know I would be late. She asked me to do my best to be on time because Francis liked people to be there for the outline of his retreat. Imagine one whole week where I would be nurtured both physically and spiritually.

I had the good fortune to have a room of my own because I booked it the moment I received the brochure. I also had the space to reflect on my own life through the contents of the retreat. The weather was fantastic which meant total freedom to do and be. I missed the first session. I sat in the kitchen with a cup of tea waiting for the group to emerge from the conference room. The first through the door was Francis. What struck me at first was the fact he was Indian. With a name like P. J. Francis I thought he was Western. His eyes connected with mine as he greeted me. There was a strong feeling that I recognised them from before, yet I had never met the man. "The good wine came last!" I blurted out, shocked I had uttered these words. I had seven days to explore every feeling that emerged.

The biggest problem I had to deal with was finding the balance in my understanding of service. Even though I had come through so much, the need to be liked was still colouring my relationships. The problem was not that I didn't see clearly, it was having the energy and courage to deal with displeasing others when necessary. I was tired coping with life.

After each session I headed back to write and in the afternoon I walked through the forest. This reflection time was necessary. I definitely still had a problem. Having had to find a voice in the preceding years I thought I had come far enough. I really hadn't, even though I had made progress. I had no clear list of priorities for me and it was easy to lose track of what was important. My needs were muddled up in everyone else's. I recognised my old enemy, guilt. I spent my life responding to what life threw at me instead of taking responsibility for what I wanted from life. Spiritual people didn't do this was my perception. My week in Chrysalis ousted some of my most destructive beliefs.

When I got diabetes that Christmas it was at the end of a long run of faith that someway or other I would emerge from this mire. Some part of me felt as I lay on that hospital bed that I was being punished. I was doing and responding in every way I knew through awareness. Anthony de Mello said, "Once you are bitten by the bug of awareness there is no going back!" I really wondered if I was better off fully asleep as I used to be. I could see that some improvement had been made on detachment. I did not feel totally responsible for the happiness of others. I was much more skilled at helping others see how they had a part in what was happening to them. Before I would have been on full alert taking over their problem! As much as it was tempting to stop I knew there was no going back to the blame game.

Francis returned to Chrysalis in July 2000. I repeated the programme. This time I was a bit more open and I talked to him about the work I was doing on myself. I explained to him how I saw Awareness working in my home, and in the school. I was more interested in applied awareness. Of what use would awareness be to me if it remained solidly in my head. "Who am I?" was the question. "Why are we here?" Spiritual beings having a human existence! To have that experience of being totally connected to your spirit while you are living a mortal life, while you deal with day to day living, now that is the challenge. When you strip away false beliefs, beliefs based on beliefs of others who have not experienced what they are talking about, it is the beginning of seeing reality.

I found time to speak to Francis during the week. He had known Anthony de Mello personally and it helped bring some perspective of Anthony as a human being. Awareness did not happen to Anthony overnight. He, too, had to go through this process of stripping away. Francis said that of all the thousands who listened to Anthony perhaps only a handful ever put awareness into practise. Awareness had become an intellectual experience.

I had spent many years searching through various therapies and courses and was no better off, but with Awareness I knew where to look, it was like it had given me a shovel and spade and put me to work, not on other people but on myself. It wasn't preachy! Life was easily lived in the nurturing environment of Chrysalis. I loved the meditations and the peace I experienced daily. Yet I was anxious. My anxiousness had to do with facing the unknown. Where would all this change take me? Paddy McMahon

(Patrick Francis) told me in 1994 that I would teach Awareness. This was unsettling. Why was I slow to acknowledge this? The root was fear. If I proceeded to move fully into Awareness, then I might be pushed to share it. That would take me away from my family. The only thing to do with fear is to face it and move through it. Not to move through it would be to give the mind dominance. My experience was that people were not particularly interested in my painstaking approach to self-awareness. It was too practical and it all seemed too ordinary. People want to escape from reality. Reality can be exhausting.

One afternoon we were all quietly listening to Francis as he slowly read a Loving Kindness meditation. We were asked to think of various situations and fill each one with loving kindness no matter how difficult they appeared to be. He moved in the meditation to people in our lives whom we loved. Then he moved to the people who caused us pain. To each one we were asked to fill them with loving kindness. The man beside me began to laugh until his whole being rocked. He did his best to conceal it. Later in the evening I asked him what happened. He said that he could see this person who was a thorn in his side. He thought of how lovely it would be if he could do this meditation; fill this lady with loving kindness. Only when he had finished visualising did he realise what he was saying. Instead of silently saying, "May you be filled with loving kindness," he was saying, "May you be free from loving kindness." The subconscious mind is an interesting place. Deep within us is a canyon that contains the best and the worst of us. Quietness allows it surface! When we fear, we busy ourselves. When we get fed up living in fear we have nothing to lose, then it is called being sick of our sickness, and we really don't care what emerges so long as it does and we see what is controlling us. That is Awareness!

Francis needed to return to Dublin after the course. I offered to take him. I somehow expected it to be a long uncomfortable journey back. I can be quite shy but I did want to hear more about

Anthony. I had experienced the spiritual Francis during the retreat, now I wanted to see the ordinary Francis. Where was he actually in relation to Awareness? The Francis who had to face the challenges of being Director of Sadhana Institute! Francis in ordinary relationships! We spoke of the challenge of living awareness. That not to be able to blame another human being for our unhappiness at times seemed extreme. I was sick of giving out, sick of moaning, sick of feeling resentful. It was time for change. Anthony said that even if I practised Awareness for three weeks there would be change! It was true, change happened yet the constant observation and analysis of my own reactions was quite tiring. I needed to take time out daily in nature, a local park or beach to keep my spirits raised. I saw too that Francis had work to do. This made it easier for me to talk to him. When you put people on pedestals, though they may never ask to be put on one, invariably as you get to know them they tumble down. Your expectations of them get in the way of the relationship. I didn't want to put him on one. That was why it was important for me to speak to him on that journey. I left Francis with his friend and thought that was it. I knew that the following year his retreat was scheduled for June so that would rule me out as the school closed at the end of June.

I had just bought a computer and was learning how to use email. I thought about writing to him in July but was very reticent. Somehow I felt it would be good to wait. At the end of August, I sent him a thank you email. I was sorry I would not be returning for another course but was content with what I had received. I got a reply about a week later. He had been asking if anyone had an email address for me. He was very interested in how I approached Awareness and could see it would be helpful for him in marrying spirituality, clinical psychology and daily living outside the confines of a spiritual order. He could see that psychology, like religion can only bring people to a door. They must choose to go the rest of the way. He knew my practical approach would greatly support him in earthing his spirituality. It was the beginning of us working together online.

Why do bad things happen to kind people? Sometimes it happens to push them beyond the narrow confines of their beliefs about themselves. Why do people take advantage of kind people? Perhaps to push them to the wall to wake up. Why are the needs of helpful people ignored? Perhaps overzealous people do not respect their own needs!

CHAPTER 19

A Passage to India

**'Our doubts are traitors, and make us lose the
good we might oft win by fearing to attempt'**
William Shakespeare

BLESS technology! Having Francis who understood awareness was helpful. We supported each other on self-awareness through reflection on daily happenings. Only through this could either of us identify where and why and how we added to the disturbance in our lives. From a distance we had the detachment necessary to help each other out. As I shared my experience of how I worked out my part in the difficulties I faced, and also with clarity began to see where I needed to take a step back and allow others the opportunity of finding their own solutions, he began to see how this could work as a workshop. Where was Awareness taking me? One part of me wanted a simple life, another part of me felt that I hadn't even begun to live life. The simple life was a desire to keep our family life uncomplicated. I wanted to be around for my children as they progressed. The desire within me to do something more with my life also burned like a flame. That was my disturbance!

Francis asked if I would travel to India. There was a Vipassana meditation course in April and he felt it would benefit me. This course would require me to be silent in a small room while guided by a facilitator. There would be no communication either during rest times. I felt, if this could take me to a deeper level of Awareness, then I was all for it. If I chose to make the trip, I could only take ten days' maximum during my Easter Holidays. Part of me wanted to experience where Anthony de Mello had lived. I could visualise myself in the garden where he taped his last meditations. The whole idea was exciting. If I was the only one affected, then there would have been no obstacles. What about leaving the children? The usual doubts emerged. The next was the selfishness of spending that much money on me. We had many needs at the time and this was not on a priority list. My fiftieth birthday was coming up and I really did want to do something for me.

Francis could not see any restrictions. It was simple to him. This was only going to be for two weeks so what was my problem? I made enquiries with the Travel agent and the tickets were expensive. He had absolutely no idea how difficult it was for me financially at that time. As a Jesuit he was shielded from that reality. I reached another wall. I see Jim Carey in that film "The Truman Show". To keep him controlled, family, friends and neighbours played on his fears. To control anyone, you play on their fears! Did I want to be controlled, did I want my children to be controlled by irrational fear? Ultimately I was the one who had to choose. Part of me also wanted an excuse not to go because I was terrified of flying. I had never ever gone on an airplane for more than four hours. This one required stop overs and at least eight hours flying time. I had never had to find my way through strange airports on my own. The bottom line was my fear of the unknown. I clung to the known. Sink or swim? Another person in my situation with a different perception or experience would have no qualms. There is only one way to change your world and that is to change your perception of it. I took a deep breath and booked the tickets.

Paul got very sick. Why now? He was the healthiest of the crew. He had a cough similar to whooping cough. I brought him to the hospital for tests but they could not find anything unusual. This cough had gone on for weeks and he was out of school. I had hoped it would be better before I left. I had heard of an old wife's tale that if a child had whooping cough you should take them to the ocean. If you walked in and out of the water seven times it would heal. What had we to lose? It also gave us some quality time together walking the beach. On the way back he spoke of his wish to learn how to drive a car. I was reluctant saying that I loved this little machine of mine and I was afraid to risk anything happening to it. We took the scenic route home, driving through Enniskerry in Co. Wicklow. Along the way a football came rolling out across the road. Being used to the behaviours of children I expected to see a child come running after it and I braked. The instantaneous crash into our car pushed us forward violently. I was thankful that I was capable of getting out of the car but what I saw shocked me. The rear of the car was sitting on the back seat. My first thought was gratitude that Annie did not come with us. She certainly would either have been killed or badly injured. There was no escape for her there. Paul, like me, got whiplash and it didn't help his existing back trouble. The driver of the other vehicle was a foreign national and hadn't sufficient English to communicate. The police arrived and took the details as did the Ambulance men. No one in the other car was even slightly injured. Sorting out this problem took three years as the other driver had no tax or insurance and now I had no car. The AA association brought the remnants of mine back to the house and told me the car was written off. There was no point in repairing it. I telephoned the insurance agency and was told that I was not entitled to its actual value. I had to leave dealing with it until I got back. Not having a car meant I could not go chasing around trying to do too much before I left. Whatever I could do I did and had to be content with that. I kept looking for signs to see if I was doing the right thing by going. This accident and Paul being sick were not helping. Finally, the day for departure arrived. Paul stayed up all night to make sure I would have some sleep but also to wake me up on time. The taxi came at 3.30 am. My poor dog McNabb was not happy. She followed me up the stairs, down the stairs and through every room. She went out to stand by the taxi. The taxi driver said, "Could someone take that dog away. I can't look at her. She looks so sad." It was true. She had been following me for days.

The first part through Dublin airport went smoothly. Next challenge was Amsterdam and again there were no problems. I felt relieved when I boarded the second plane as next stop was Bombay. Nearer our destination we were handed an immigration form. I looked at it and saw a section for a visa number. Not being familiar with this I assumed it was for people who were staying long term. The travel agent didn't say anything to me and it never occurred to me that I needed one. I thought they would give me one on arrival if I needed one. Coming in to land was spectacular. The extraordinary mix of colourful lights was exciting. Everything seemed so different. The air hostess called my name along with some others. There was a sign when we disembarked and I went over to the attendants. My luggage had been left in Amsterdam. They told me not to worry as it would arrive the following day. There were corrals to separate the people as we moved towards immigration. At least three flights had come in at the same time so there was a large crowd. The officials were moving quickly and soon it came to my turn. He looked disdainfully at the passport. There was no sign of animation on his face. Then he asked the question, "Where is your visa?" I replied that I didn't have one, that I was only here on holiday. My reply really pissed him off. How did I think I could enter the country without a visa? I was shocked. What could I do? I asked if I could get one at the Embassy. This sent him into a rage. He demanded I wait there. He got up from his seat and called another officer.

Another official arrived! The same questions! Where was my visa? I explained again. This did not seem to satisfy them. They talked among themselves. For a moment I felt that it would be sorted. The full implications were not apparent to me. I knew you did not need a visa for New Zealand or Japan or even America. You could sign a visa form on the airplane. I was questioned over and over until finally they decided that I was to return home. I asked if I could telephone Francis. "No". I asked if I could telephone my family. "No". I was handed a boarding pass and told to wait there and board the next flight. They would not let me out of their sight. Finally, two officers left and I waited with a junior officer. He brought me to a telephone and I phoned home. Grace answered and I told her that I was on my way home from Bombay. She got very upset for me. I hadn't enough time to digest what was happening. I was numb.

I was assigned a place in the front of the plane beside families with small children. The television screen loomed in front of me. The film was "What Women Want." I thought, "A visa!" This was my first long journey with diabetes. I had managed so far, what was to happen on the way back? Despite everything I slept. I blocked everything out. It was totally out of my control. I got to Amsterdam and enquired about my luggage. They told me it was in Bombay. I felt winded. The air was out of my system and I could hardly breathe. Right! What to do? Firstly, I telephoned Francis. I told him I had been in touch with Grace and she was enquiring about a visa. The Indian Embassy told her that if I went in to them on Monday they would sort it out for me. I hoped to be travelling back on Wednesday. I said I would let him know as soon as I contacted the Travel Agent. I felt quite calm.

I went in search of an Aer Lingus desk. I heard a last boarding call for Dublin. I ran towards the desk and they said it was too late for me to catch that flight and there wouldn't be another until the following day. There was a strike on Friday with Aer Lingus. She apologised for the inconvenience. This was inconvenience even to well experienced travellers. For me, it was like being plummeted into hell. I actually felt terror for the first time since I began the journey. Where was I to go, what could I do? I noticed a queue outside a tourist information desk.

When it came to my turn the lady said that it was very difficult to find accommodation in Amsterdam. There were many events happening that weekend. I prayed that I would find something. If there was a God up there, then surely He or She would see my plight. She found a hotel near a railway station. She suggested that I go on the train. I was too tired and stressed to even try and understand foreign train timetables. I knew I would be totally lost, yet I feared if I got into a taxi it would be the last seen of me. I must have watched too many crime movies. I settled for the taxi. The driver seemed pleasant enough and I had to trust he would take me to where I was going. Then he stopped the car and told me that it was too complicated with one way streets to drive to the hotel door. "What am I to do" I asked him? He said, "Walk". "Walk to where?" He dismissed me like I was some nuisance fly. I got out with my hand luggage and walked in the general direction, asking people along the way. I had little luck as most had no English. When I did see the Hotel I was very relieved. I booked in and went to my room. It was a simple, clean room with no natural light. I didn't care. I could lie down and absorb what was happening. I rested and took a shower and went down to the foyer. I asked the manager what time dinner started. He abruptly said that Amsterdam was full of restaurants but they did not have one. They supplied breakfast and that was all.

It was getting towards evening and dark. The only reason I moved out was that I had to eat. I did not have enough food for my diabetes. I walked through the streets, hoping not to appear too obviously on my own and found a small restaurant. I felt alone and abandoned. That lasted about half an hour. I was seated near a window and noticed the people walking by. None seemed too enamoured with life though they were in company. With that I ordered a glass of the finest wine and contented myself. I was alone but not lonely. I found gazing out the window had its merits. I could safely watch the world go by. The meal was delicious and when I finally settled the bill, I strolled happily back to the hotel.

I thought about my experience and felt we can either choose to have our glass half empty or half full. As I lay there thinking about it I did not recognise this person who had come through so many scrapes. She was not the person who set out on this journey. I had an option. I could stay in the hotel in the morning or I could explore Amsterdam on the money that I had set aside for the Vipassana retreat. I could lose myself in meditation or find myself in life!

Meditation would have been a cop out and an excuse for this fearful person. Life won hands down. I booked to go on one of the canal tours and also to take a tram ride to Anne Frank's house. I thought I would be covered by insurance. Ignorance is bliss!

I met a lovely young girl from Ukraine. Her name was Oxana. She was in Amsterdam to work and was taking some time out to meet her friend? she met her friend who was a journalist. We sailed down the canals. I was mesmerised by the architecture and how we had similar examples in Dublin. It was the Huguenot influence. How insular we were in Ireland before we travelled. We did not see how connected we were to the outer world. Oxana and I got on very well and she invited me to join her for the day. My flight was not until late evening. We met up with her friend on Dam Square and he told me he was a journalist. He took his role as tour guide seriously and immediately took us to the Red light district. I had heard of this before and had seen a programme on television about this area. Fresh in my mind was an image of a lady with the most enormous breasts sitting in a window saying she lured men with her eyes. We strolled through the streets. We had been warned as teenagers that if ever we went to this area it would mean certain hell. The flames would burn brighter for such escapades. We sat in a pub and had a coffee. There was a peculiar smell there and I was happy to get out into the fresh air. When I told Michelle and Grace about the strange smell later they cried laughing. "Mum, it was weed!"

They walked me back to Dam Square and I knew my way back to the hotel to collect my hand luggage. I was really glad of the experience. A taxi brought me to the airport and once he knew my destination he knew the terminal. It was all quite simple but to the uninitiated it was daunting.

Though I was disappointed at my turnaround I also found coming into Dublin welcoming. There is something beautiful about the landing. Howth in front of you and a glimmer of Ireland's eye! The land is so green and lush that you cannot but be impressed by it all. I had an easy journey home in the end where I was met by all of my gang. They had planned to put up a banner welcoming the deportee home but thought the better of it. Paul managed to get released from homework claiming trauma. His cheesy grin telling the story made a lie of that one. I suppose at age sixteen you need to get some mileage out of the events. Annie painted a really lovely picture of a Buddhist Temple and bought a tea light holder for me. She knew how much this journey meant to me and was sad at how it all turned out. Grace had already made enquiries about visa applications and had all the required documentation ready for me. Michelle had looked after the brood well.

The next day I went to the travel agent and explained my predicament. Grace had already spoken to Edel who was extremely helpful. Edel, looking at the flight information asked me for the second part of my ticket. "Which part?" I enquired. "The part from Amsterdam to Bombay," she replied. I told her I landed in Bombay. I had gone through interrogation and was flown back on the next available flight. Her expression was priceless. This changed everything. The only plus in all of it was that my planned return flight was still in the system so that meant only finding a flight out.

Amazed at my calmness the manageress came over and said that this time there would be no travel agent's charge. I did appreciate that as I took out my MasterCard to pay for the flight. I was not entitled to any insurance as I was responsible for the visa and it was in the small print. I hadn't been told to look out for that but in this day and age perhaps they did not think of saying it because most travellers would have known.

I then went to the Indian Embassy. They were a bit confused as to how I got past the checks in Amsterdam. After much questioning they did fast forward the visa application and had it ready for Tuesday. I departed on Wednesday. Was it a case of good luck bad luck, who knows? Every step of that journey made me reflect on fears and limitations being created at breakneck speed. Each one came up for reflection and for each one I could create a conscious choice. This energised me and took me out of victim mode.

I had a later return flight so no early morning departure. I strolled up to the bus stop with Grace and Annie. Annie was on her way to school so it gave us time to be together. My main luggage was already in Bombay. Sitting at the airport this time around I wondered was I doing the right thing returning to India. The manic preparations hid the underlying anxieties and every one of them came up for review. As I sat down for a cup of coffee with Grace and poured my confused thoughts out at her she marched me over to the departure gates and as much as pushed me through. I was more or less made eat my own words as she laughingly said, "Stop your bloody nonsense!"

When asked for my visa in Amsterdam I looked at the man like a rabbit in the headlights. "Phew," I got through. At least he checked. Next stop Bombay. Approaching landing my heart was in my mouth. What if it isn't enough? I moved slowly in the queue with a racing heart. I could hear the loud stamp as another passport was accepted.

My turn came. I seemed to have developed verbal diarrhoea explaining where my visa page was and my excitement at being there. It was wasted on his expressionless, bored countenance. He opened the passport slowly, looked at all the pages slowly, not even a mildly friendly expression on the face. A grunt, a stamp and I was handed the passport. I walked through. I did have documentation for my luggage and they went to a room nearby to bring out the case. I took one look at this grey and battered case and wanted to disown it. As all my goods and chattels were inside it, I could do nothing but put it up on the trolley. I went in the direction of the customs officials. Everything was put through another scanner before leaving and I walked out into the clammy warm air. It was a sea of people, standing behind barriers. The noise of cars, horns, auto rickshaws, and people shouting assailed me. This was two thirty in the morning and it was like midday traffic.

I searched through the array of colour to see if there was a banner with my name on it. Then I saw it. This lovely friendly guy came towards me and took care of the trolley. He had some English so I asked if it were possible to phone home. I was told in Dublin that my sim card would work. I had paid for roaming charges in advance but it was no good. He showed me where I could make a call. They have many stands where if you give the number they will dial it for you and will charge you very little to make a phone call. I was delighted to tell everyone that I had arrived and was met.

I expected the streets to be empty at that hour of the morning. I also expected it to be cooler with the mosquitoes in bed. They came out in their hoards to greet me. Whatever blood type I have, they love it. It wasn't helped by my ignorance around the habits of mosquitoes; they are attracted to perfume. The multi-coloured trucks were out in full force with a message on the back that said "Sound the Horn". It is expected that you beep and it was clear it was normal because of the incessant honking. I sat in the back of the 4x4 and accepted the fact there were no seatbelts as we drove out from the airport. Sleeping bodies on the pavements, vendors still selling, dogs roaming around, were all part of their normal life.

My suspicious mind had me thinking, "Where is he taking me?" I was glad to see a sign for Lonavla. I relaxed and looked at the scenery. Though I was tired, my delight at being in India and whisking my way through the countryside kept me wide awake. At times we were completely stuck in traffic jams, bumper to bumper as we made our way slowly up the hills. Lonavla is a hill station and is surrounded by beautiful scenery. Though it is only about one hundred kilometres to Sadhana it took many hours to reach it. This was a time before the expressway opened to Pune. It is an easier journey now. When we got to the gate and I saw the Sadhana sign my heart filled. I had made it.

Tired and weary I got out of the vehicle. I hadn't expected

Sadhana to be so big, going by the descriptions of people who had previously attended; neither did I expect the building to look so modern. As I made my way through the front doors into the hallway I noticed a large picture of Anthony on the wall. I sat on the couch available and waited for Francis to arrive. In the meantime, the driver took my bags in for me.

It was seven in the morning and the place was buzzing with course participants. They silently walked by, smiling at me. I wondered at their silence, completely forgetting that Vipassana means they cannot talk at all during the day. It was a silent retreat.

Francis arrived and greeted me. I was also warmly welcomed by Sister Selma. Selma knew Anthony through the years and was a very good friend of his. I was shown to my room and told I had a shower also. It was hot and humid I could not wait to have that shower. I looked for dials to select water temperature. There were none. It was a cold shower. I silently screamed as the water hit me but I didn't have any option. This was it. I never did get used to that one. There was a long pole at the end of the bed. I had no idea what that was for. I found out on the last day it was to hang the mosquito net!.

I went down to the dining room for breakfast. One large long table with many varieties of food was available. I had not eaten Indian food before and wondered how I would get on. It makes my mouth water to even think of it now. Each and every curry was amazing. The girls were lovely cooks and Selma kept an eye on operations to make sure that standards were high. They would scuttle passed you smiling as they went about their work. I had no Hindi or Marathi and they had no English. Interesting how you can communicate without language.

Once I settled in I was free to explore. Francis and Selma had a very busy schedule and I made my way up to the old Villa where Anthony ran Sadhana for a few years before moving into the new buildings. These buildings seemed to be in need of repair but judging by old accounts they were always in need of repair. They were set among the trees. I walked up a path from the new Sadhana Institute building to the old. There was a very old stone wall, and set inside it was an iron gate. To me it looked a bit like the Secret Garden. I opened the gate and stepped inside. There was what looked like an old bandstand where you could sit, but I moved beyond there up the pathway and through the trees. There were seats dotted here and there. The pervading sound was of the crickets in the trees and in the nearby property the street children, who were on vacation from Bombay happily sweeping leaves from the area in preparation for their cricket games.

I sat on a bench each day meditating. The only obstacle for me was the mosquito. They must have rejoiced seeing me when I arrived because they made an instant feast of my blood. The jungle formula spray I brought with me was of little use. Thankfully I did bring a special cream for bites otherwise I would more than likely have ended up in hospital.

I needed this time for myself. It was easy for insights into my own life to come up for me in the quietness. Perhaps sitting under those trees on the seat where Anthony used to sit gave me a sense of the place. No one interrupted me. I was free to go and come as I pleased. I returned for meal times.

The Vipassana retreat was not for me that time. I saw the group enter the room early morning and emerge silently before meals. They walked in silence through the gardens. I hadn't really thought about what it entailed. Francis had recommended it to me and I went along with that. The Universe must have thought otherwise because I was put through a million learning lessons in order to avoid that experience. It you want to make God laugh make plans. Every plan of mine was scuppered. Hindsight is wonderful because not one part of it all would I change now.

We all gathered together at mealtimes. We nodded to each other. I sat at a table with Francis, Selma and the facilitator. Silence activates your senses. I noticed the body language of the facilitator and asked Francis later, "Is he an angry man?" "What would make you think that?" "The way he handles his fork. His general body language would indicate a very rigid person."

He looked the part of the spiritual teacher in his movements but there was something missing. It seemed unnatural. This man was both respected and revered by the group. Francis asked as to how I could come to this conclusion when I knew nothing about him and I had not been in the place twenty-four hours. "Body language, his gaze," I replied. He smiled.

Being in the fresh air meditating was a better choice for me. Every day I relished the open air. I am not the adventurous type, so setting off on my own to the local town didn't entice me. I still had to get used to the volume of people, the craziness of drivers, the movement of goats, dogs, bulls and sometimes elephants sharing the same street. On one occasion I witnessed a mahout on a mobile phone on top of an elephant. Anything is possible in India. Another day, I saw in the middle of Bombay a bull leisurely stroll across the street. No one except me batted an eyelid.

In the morning after breakfast I walked down the steps towards the villa. I was greeted by Mama the gardener. "Namaste!" he would say and join his hands. His eyes gleamed as he looked at me. The genuine welcome always touched me. Mama only spoke Marathi, so there was no hope of either of us understanding each other. How he looked and how he greeted me left me under no doubt that his welcome was pure. Something about his simplicity, the smile, his eyes were pure love. I thought about it all. We go searching here and there for love, for God, and right under our noses in places we do not expect to meet God, He is there. I had no doubt but Mama in his way of being was an expression of God. I came to find God in Vipassana and found Him in this simple man. The gift was beyond words. No mask, no affectation, just simplicity. God is to be found in the grain of the mustard seed, in the eyes of a simple gardener. I observed him with others, the girls from the kitchen, Joseph the general fixer of all things and with each one he was the same. I looked out my window one day and saw him breaking down elephant dung for the garden and happily working away as if he had the most important job in the world. He was doing what big Father asked him to do. Big Father was Francis.

When the day was over I had an opportunity to speak with Francis. It was good to share what I was thinking and feeling. Both he and Selma were extremely kind to me and they took time out to bring me to the local town, Lonavla.

Selma knowing, I wanted some saris took me to a special shop. She knew what she was about and was able to communicate with the shop owner what I was looking for. We left our shoes at the door and walked in. There were big mattresses covered with white cotton. We sat down and waited. The man took out ream after ream and threw them with great aplomb on the floor. They had been in rolls and I could see the amount of work this was causing. It didn't matter. They were used to this. I was in a sea of colour, totally mesmerised. Selma having a better idea on fabric quality, and what would work, helped me choose. As it was coming up to my fiftieth birthday and the girls were organising an Indian party for me I needed to get at least ten saris. The princely sum of about twenty euros was the amount it cost. We walked through the streets taking in the sounds and smells.

An old man was sitting with a group of friends and he spoke to Selma. He had a bowl of sweets and he offered me one. I asked Selma what he had said to her, and she replied that he had thanked her for bringing God to the community. This is traditional Indian hospitality and it is how they think of newcomers to the area. India is another world and I am not fooled in imagining I will ever fully comprehend the vastness of thought, language, politics, land, poverty, richness, and architecture. So much emphasis is given to the poverty in India, and poverty is real, but not enough understanding is given to the depth and complexity of India. Its cultural, spiritual, architectural, political and intellectual side can be ignored in Western society. India is like that ancient story Six

Blind Wise Men and an Elephant. Each blind man could sense some aspect of what an elephant looked like but their perception was based on whatever part of the elephant they touched. We can make assumptions about India but our understanding can only be limited.

Sitting on the mat choosing saris I was asked all sorts of personal questions. Selma told me this is not nosiness as such but interest and curiosity. They ask everyone such questions. Asking you what you had for breakfast was not considered invasive. Why was I there? Was I married? Where was my husband? Did I have any children? Why did I leave them? Selma was my interpreter. She said this was normal questioning, they did not mean to be rude. I loved it. I loved the honesty of it.

Francis needed to go to Pune and asked if I would like to go with him. He had some meetings and if I was prepared to put up with that then I was welcome. I wanted to go on an Indian train.

We went down to the town and he got the tickets. This is not an ordinary town by western standards. Always crowds moving here and there. The train station was no exception. Before I knew it Francis was heading at great speed towards the train. I couldn't see him. I knew if he needed to find me it wouldn't be a problem. I could not identify him in the crowds. I had to run to catch up.

Lonavla may have been bad but Pune was another challenge altogether. You take your life in your hands as you cross the road. Auto rickshaws, jeeps, cars, bicycles were all competing for space. I saw a legless man making his way across one of the busiest streets on a skate board. How anyone could see him at that level I do not know but he managed. There was no order and yet in all that chaos there was some kind of order. They seemed to know where they were going or what to expect. I would have been demolished if I had thought of driving there. To them I would be a nuisance with my need for lanes, signals and speed.

I ate my first masala dosa in a local restaurant. I asked Francis for something light as I needed to be able to calculate sugar levels. This enormous object arrived on a plate with some curries beside it. He assured me it was small and I needed to break it down. It did collapse easily but small it was not. There is absolutely no harm in it he said. What I was seeing and he was seeing was coming from two completely different lenses.

His ability to move quickly between the crowds would have worked that lot off in minutes. I got the message and chased after him, keeping his head in view. Why didn't I get a phone number from him so that I could have contacted someone in the event I got lost? I needed to exchange some money. This was a major operation. I thought it would be simple like in Ireland. I was taken to an office. A huge ledger was taken out. My passport was needed. Each transaction was recorded. I remember these ledgers in the Ulster Bank in the early seventies. It was really only because Francis was with me that this exchange was effortless. Francis bought a coconut drink for me. The vendor sliced the top off the coconut with what looked like a machete. Then he placed a straw inside it and handed it to me. It was like nectar.

The train was a real novelty. It did not rely heavily on comfort. On the roof were handles for holding on to when the train was full, which was always. The seats were wooden; the windows had bars on them to prevent gate crashers.

Looking out the window I could see the ladies working in the fields. The vividness of colour is outstanding. Along the roadsides they worked, placing stones, or gravel in tin bowls and walking towards the other workers with this on their heads. Each one of them had beautiful posture. Years of walking with cans, baskets, or tin bowls on their heads gave them a grace that I envied. Nuns used to make us walk with a book on our heads to develop a straight spine. These women had it naturally.

The week passed by too quickly. I went for a final walk in the gardens before leaving. I wanted to remember every sound, image and feeling. Bags were packed to the brim and already loaded into the jeep. It was the golden years of travelling when not much was said to you for having eight kilos over the limit. I got into the jeep and headed to the airport wondering if I would return. I wanted to be home with my family but I also wanted to come back.

Certain images come to mind as I remember that journey to the airport. I could see the long distance train making its way up the hill with a shunter engine pushing it. This train to Lonavla needed this because of the steepness of the hills and once it made its destination the shunter engine went back towards Bombay.

We stopped at a friend's apartment in Bombay. Eustace was an artist and he lived on Perry Road. His housekeeper Mary cooked a delicious meal for us. He was never short of words and illustrated his life story in detail. Eustace would take one street boy into his home with the purpose of educating him and setting him up in life. Once established in work he would help another young boy. His house was generally full of former street children who were visiting. As my flight was at 2am I was allowed lie down in the guest room for some sleep. This was very welcome before we made the final journey to the airport. I said goodbye to Francis and wondered if our paths would meet again in India. A huge part of my heart was in India. I had never been touched by a place so profoundly. Perhaps it is in my DNA. Going back a few generations my mother's relatives had lived in India. Maybe this was the reason why.

When I got home my creative, inventive daughters set about planning my fiftieth birthday party. I was tentative about the operation. The moment I mentioned that I was even considering it, my youngest sister ordered her sari. My mother who I never expected to even come to the party was in full swing. She spent weeks getting her outfit ready. She planned this like a military operation. I couldn't back down. Grace had tea lights and flowers the entire way up the driveway, on window sills and around the house. It was like a Diwali festival. We took out the recipe books and cooked Indian fare. I found out how to put on the sari from the internet. We had great fun doing this. All of us girls were in saris.

Paul, I put in a kurta and pants. He had his white Indian hat as well. He looked like a young Nehru.

When my mother and one of my sisters arrived, I wondered at their outfits. They were dressed like characters from the British Raj. The Jewel in the Crown! My sister-in-law arrived as Indira Gandhi and my brother-in-law as a Buddhist monk. Every aspect was represented. We were a mixture of young and old having a wonderful experience. I never thought that my family would enter into the fun of this. The response was so full of vitality and this, made the day much more special than I ever thought it could be.

A few weeks later as I strolled down the road with Annie, licking an ice cream, she announced. "You know the way I said to you before Christmas that all I have to look forward to is a life like yours, where you do nothing but work? Your trip to India changed that." I said, "I will never forget that night, you cried all night." "Well, it's different now that you have gone to India. I have many things to look forward to."

I was silenced. There I was for years thinking you had to give up everything for your children. Stay at home, keep everything safe, and here she was thinking the opposite.

We take on a role and adopt a way of moving around our perception of that role. Natural inclinations are rejected when we do this. Over the years it becomes a mask we hide behind and we are unaware of it.

CHAPTER 20

The Way Forward

'The negative feeling is in you, not in reality'
Anthony de Mello

F RANCIS returned to Ireland at the end of June to facilitate a retreat at the Chrysalis Centre. He had made preparations to go to Galway to visit friends before the retreat and come to us afterwards. I had my concerns. His world was very different. How would he fit in with an ordinary Irish family complete with a dog and a cat who had rights? I was financially strapped. It was one thing to be communicating by email another to be living in the same house for a full week. I took some quiet time to myself before the visit and settled comfortably with the feeling that I would keep it simple. There was no point in creating an image that could not be sustained, neither was there any point in my having to deal with financial pain afterwards. It was important for me to be true to ourselves. Take us or leave us!

I brought him to visit the Hill of Tara which is a sacred site associated with the Kingship of Ireland and Slieve na Caillaighe an ancient megalithic tomb. The walk up the hill to the tomb always takes my breath away. The view from the top is really worth the walk. Many times I went there on my own over the years whenever I needed to clear my thoughts. You collect the key to the gate of the tomb from a local restaurant. There is a small deposit required and a stipulation that only you use the key and do not give to someone else after you. Many people failed to return the key and on one occasion some genius borrowed it and asked people for an entrance fee at the gate as a money spinner! The space inside is very confined but when you make your way across a boulder and get into the centre there is sufficient space for four people to stand. On your own this is quiet and peaceful. In March and September, the early morning sun shines directly in through the gate and lights up the whole area naturally. Even without entering the tomb the entire area is covered with the remains of smaller tombs. You can sit on top of the main one and pass the time peacefully or sit on what is known as The Hags Chair which is set into the side of the hill. Cailleach translated from Irish is Hag or Crone. Sit there and ask for the wisdom of the Crone.

Also part of the itinerary was Glendalough which has the most spectacular scenery. It is a world famous monastic site and thousands come to visit each year. We both loved the scenery, natural beauty and the quietness from the hillsides.

We walked for miles around the lakes and chatted away effortlessly. We went for a walk up the Sugar Loaf Mountain and as we neared the top a mist descended. We continued on up thinking that it would not be too heavy. The mist became very dense. As we reached the top another couple was coming down. We didn't think of following them as we were not the slightest bit concerned. I had walked this mountain before but there were always people around. It was only when we began to make the descent that we got lost. Nothing seemed familiar. We had no compass with us and it was quite scary. We continued walking down the mountain but were unsure of which direction to go. As we came through the mist we could see the road in the distance but no matter what way we tried to descend we were surrounded by thick bramble. The prickly thorns were so sharp we could not get through. This would not have been so bad if my sugar levels were not dropping and my supply of glucose running out. We tried this way and that but it was impassable.

We walked past a quarry and followed a path along the top until we came to a house. We walked through their farm yard and had to climb across railings to reach the road. The mist soaked us through and through and it was difficult for me to get across the gate as my denim jeans were stiff with water. By the time I got to the car my sugars were down to 2 and I was feeling groggy. I knew I had chocolate in the car but was so out of sync that I could not focus on where I had left it. I managed to mumble something to Francis. It was his first experience of someone heading into a diabetic coma and, he not fully understanding the reality of the situation, seemed quite calm. Ignorance is bliss! When he found the chocolate I stuffed it into my mouth quickly, sat back and waited until I could see straight. Not being able to verbalise that I was heading into a coma showed me that in relationships I still had the capacity to get lost. Perhaps that is what the mist was trying to teach me.

During the week we talked nonstop about Anthony de Mello, Sadhana's history and awareness. I couldn't believe that there was a being in the world who could understand why I was so passionate about the subject and why I felt the entire world should know about it. My understanding of myself, the changes in my life and in my family's life were so wonderful that I thought everyone should hear about Anthony and his vision. There was not enough time in the week to get all the thoughts and ideas out that had been trapped inside me for so long.

One day we went for a walk along the coastline from Malahide to Portmarnock and he bluntly told me that I spoke far too quickly. I was gutted. Here I was thinking I had found someone at last who could understand me, and here he was thinking all the time I was a babbling lunatic. Evidence again of my need for approval. I really felt shamed. "Speaking so quickly means that people are not able to hear you. You are far too intense." I was upset and dejected. Did he have to be so direct? As much as I had improved in life, I was still having a problem with criticism. I was still very vulnerable. He suggested I attend a programme at Sadhana Institute that was due to take place the following December. This course he believed would help me embody the work. It would take what I understood from my head and bring it more into my daily experience. I was taking it into my life and into my body. This remark coming from someone cocooned by the Jesuit life really got to me. My reaction was so strong I knew I needed to look deeper to find out what I was still holding onto.

The course was to be facilitated by a psychologist from America. If it could help me then I was all for it. By the time I got to India the problem was solved. I did take heed of what Francis said and in time I was able to see where it could put people off. I needed to get permission from the Board of Management to take time out from the school and bless my accommodating Principal P. J. and the chairperson of the Board of Management for granting me unpaid leave of absence. I knew that this inner work could only benefit my work with the children, so leaving them for two weeks was not going to harm them.

I headed off to India again and this time Francis met me at the airport. He spoke of his delight that I had come for this course because he had experienced its benefits personally. He observed that my speech had already slowed down remarkably well in such a short time, even before we started.

The course was mostly attended by psychologists or people in leadership positions and I found it intimidating at first. I listened carefully each day and took part in the various exercises. I learned much about my own body type. The facilitator knew nothing about any of us and yet by looking at how we stood or walked he could define our habits and behaviours. By taking note of how I moved he could see that I was slow to initiate but once engaged I became enthused. The negative aspect of being slow to engage was that I found it difficult to begin a project but once immersed in it I had difficulty finalising it. This was a time waster. I needed to be aware of this. This actually was a real problem for me. The more I thought about it the more I could see how this happened. Even if there was no one to delay me I would delay. I also know that moving from one project to another is difficult for me. I need to be present in the new before I can take it up. That even goes down to something as simple as going into town to shop. First stop has to be a coffee shop. I need to get into the zone of shopping. Then I am fully available for whatever it takes to get a good bargain.

He looked at the group and placed us into groups of likeminded energies. It was truly fascinating. For the unsuspecting individual who might not know of this peculiarity of my need for space between activities, I must appear to either be non-attentive or stubborn.

For some days I was in awe of the course at Sadhana and what the psychologist was saying. He spoke at length about the methods he employed during therapy sessions. Not being a therapist and sitting among therapists put me in a different category. I didn't like what I was hearing in one session because I felt his methods appeared to be manipulative. "There is a danger in therapy," he said, "where the client can become emotionally attached to the therapist." I am sure there are situations like that. Not being either a counsellor or a psychologist I felt we were being taught tricks, ways to protect ourselves from intrusion by the client. In this case I was seeing it from the client's point of view. I was looking for a course on personal awareness and understanding and if we were being taught ways and means of protecting ourselves, which can be helpful but which does not go to a deeper level of understanding, then we were moving away from what I had hoped to achieve on this course.

My purpose for being present was different. I was looking for awareness in relationships. This role play appeared to be showing where the problem was with the client which was the direct opposite to what Anthony de Mello was teaching. The client could have a problem, but if the therapist had to go into all sorts of game playing to protect him or herself, then they also had a problem. What was their role in this?

I thought of Anthony and how he was so free. No one would have been able to manipulate him. I was more interested in awareness and understanding why I was easily manipulated. What behaviours of mine could leave me open to being hurt? Did I trust people too much? I know I had a naïve belief around people. Why would they want to hurt anyone? Anthony was clear on this point. He said that people act out of self-interest. This is reality. Although I would have loved to deny it, I could see he was right. What hurt me most in life was always trying to please people who were very difficult to please. In this, I was also working out of self-interest. I needed their approval.

This came home to me clearly one day as I returned from school totally wiped out. Anyone with an eye in their head would see that I was exhausted. Yet one of my children asked if I would give her a lift to the bus stop. I said, "Do you not see I am exhausted? How can you ask me to do this when you are quite capable of walking?" She smiled. "You know you can always say no, and for me it is always worth a try." If I brought her to the bus stop, I too, would have been acting out of self-interest, my interest to keep her good opinion of me. I needed approval and she needed a lift. No harm done.

I continued to listen to the facilitator waiting to hear more. If everyone else was happy with the content of the course, why should I be finding fault? Was this just my own inferiority complex? Was I being a trouble maker? If I spoke out would it be because I needed attention? Was I trying to prove I had a brain in my head? Clarity came when he mentioned in passing that he had an ability to change a client's energy. If their personality annoyed him he could do this and it made it easier for him to deal with that person. Where was the healing in this?

Again it brought me back to Anthony. If I am upset, then the upset is in me. What am I going to do with it? What is it in me that has me getting all ruffled because this person is in my company? Another person would not have any difficulty. This facilitator was using ways and means of protection but no insight into his difficulty. That was the beginning of my questioning his teaching. My reasoning was that if a client comes to me to have a problem sorted and I am changing their energy because I am uncomfortable, then there is something wrong with me. If I do not see this and I am the psychologist, then there is no way I can help this person unless I am fully aware of this.

At the beginning of the course he had said that if anyone had any questions to feel free to ask. I had listened attentively for about four days and when I did ask I shot three pertinent questions at him. He didn't like it and made some reference to my being a trouble maker and there that was always one in every group. From then on whatever I did or said was evidence to him of my belligerence. If we were asked a question and I did not reply in the manner he liked, then he would point it out to the group as another example. I began to doubt myself at first but then I knew I needed to trust my intuition that there was something amiss in what he was teaching. He originally said that we could choose to work with whatever partner we liked but then he changed his mind and placed me with a very strong psychologist and told him that he should not allow me speak to him because I would have his soul by Tuesday. I was a manipulator. I thought this was a bit over the top. The barrage was relentless and I found myself on an embodying experience that I had not envisaged for myself. So it came to the end of the programme and each one was asked what they had gained. I quietly prayed before I was asked and declared, "I now know that I am not afraid to speak even in very difficult circumstances." He looked as if he could combust on the spot.

Whether he liked it or not, he had to put up with my company in the jeep as we were both catching a plane at about the same time? He must have realised that he had burned his bridges because he became smarmy and sweet just before our departure. I was not taken in. Though he behaved in this way he was one of the best teachers that I have experienced. I also realised that it is vitally important to recognise what is important and true for you and to stay by that truth once you have discerned it. As Paddy McMahon said years earlier, "Hail the irker as he is your teacher." The course was very important for me. I needed to bring more authority into my body, I needed to be able to ask questions without fearing the consequences, I needed to learn ways of asking so that I could be heard and I realised that I am not responsible for the feelings that emerge in another. That was his to discover. It was some ten days.

It's not that we fear the unknown. You cannot fear something that you do not know. What we fear is the loss of the known or the return of pain from our past.

CHAPTER 21

The Drug
of Approval

'God is not attained by process of addition
to the soul but by subtraction'

Meister Eckhart

IT was my elderly friend Marie who introduced me to the
work of Anthony de Mello many years previously. She had
invited me, my husband and his mother to a meal with old friends
of hers. There was a heated discussion about this fellow de Mello
and I was fascinated at how animated they were. When I went to
Sadhana and brought back some photographs she was anxious to
go too. I contacted her before Christmas when I was in India
attending the Embodying Experience and I asked her if she could
take a look at flights around Easter time. She was really excited.
I knew this was vitally important to her so I took out a loan to fund
my costs for the trip.

My close friend Kate was also interested and she said she would
help me take care of her. Francis was clear when he said that if she
did not come at that time, it was quite possible that he would not
be in Sadhana and therefore, it might be her last chance to do this.
As I was still in India she went to town immediately and booked
flights for all three of us for the following Easter. I felt indebted to
her for her help and friendship throughout the years. This was her
dream. She was a seasoned traveller so I had no concerns and she
was going to be well looked after in Sadhana.

Nearing the time, I happened to be in her home for a meal with
some of her friends and I noticed she never mentioned her
upcoming trip. In fact, she seemed quite uneasy when the topic
arose about my previous trip. There was something odd about it
all. I asked later if everything was alright and she said there was

nothing amiss. I approached her to finalise the booking and she got very upset. She said her friends and family were very much against the trip and she didn't know what to do. I emphasised that this was a chance in a million and something she always wished for. I also said that only she could make the decision but if she denied herself this opportunity based on others fears, or if she feared what they would think about her should she decide to go, then this was essentially her difficulty. Not an easy one at her age and I had to leave her decide.

She decided against the trip citing many excuses but I knew she was saddened. Her sadness had more to do with not being able to move through her fears around upsetting people and, that she did need their help and it could have jeopardised their friendship. They would have gotten over it in time. The drug of approval can be costly. She knew that I would not hold this against her, so our friendship was intact and always remained so.

Kate and I went on ahead. It was to be a wonderful trip. We arrived at the front door of Sadhana at some unearthly hour of the morning. The door was opened by Brother Prakash, the administrator. He presented himself in a shirt and lungi, which is a piece of cloth that covered the lower part of his body. His hair was like a wild bush and he was very happy to see Father return from the airport with his two Irish guests. "Did I just see an apparition?" said Kate as we walked up the steps.

Prakash certainly made the trip colourful. He practised his English on us and was very happy if at any time he could correct us. Kate loved the food. This food is beautiful, she declared. Well, he raised his body to new heights, looked us both in the eye and said, "Beautiful to look at, delicious to eat." He was delighted. "Prakash, in Ireland we say 'That's gorgeous or that's beautiful.'" He was having none of it, we needed correction! Every evening he would sit with Kate and let her know about the difficulties of being the administrator. The Director literally had very little to do when he was around. Kate being truly Irish would take out another bottle of beer and allow him his illusions. He was a simple and very kind man. He had a willing ear listening to him talk of his great achievements and that made him very happy.

There were no courses going on then, so Kate and I had time to be together. Francis was busy with the running of the place between courses, so we had lots of time to explore. This was around the time of the Anthony de Mello Hall's completion. The architecture, interior design, the quality of the wood and the thought that went into the creation of the sound proof therapy rooms and meditation rooms, was precision at its best. That Easter, Francis held a Vigil in the old building and we all went over to a Mass in the new building. There were only a few of us present. We sat in a circle on cushions as we all participated. This was a very poignant moment for each of us.

Kate loved the old garden surrounding the villa and she quietly spent her time meditating whenever she got a chance. Both of us got what we needed. We strolled together down to the lake one day and got splashed with the colours of Holi. Some exuberant youths on their bicycles met with unsuspecting Irish women on their path. They were extremely happy to drown us in violet colour. Our clothes were destroyed. We laughed heartily.

Francis planned one trip away for us both at Ajanta and Ellora. Ajanta dates back to 100 BC. Ellora is younger by 600 years. The rock of Ajanta is like a giant horse shoe shape and there are at least 30 caves cut into it, all overlooking a gorge. It is unimaginable to think they were all hand cut. Chapels and temples were built for the Buddhist monks. The guide used a silver dish to demonstrate how they reflected sunlight into the cave for light to do the carvings and paintings. The existence of these caves had been unknown from 8th century AD until the 19th when they were accidentally discovered by British soldiers on manoeuvres.

Ellora was always known of as a place of pilgrimage. The most outstanding construction has to be Kailas Temple. It is the largest monolithic structure in the world. Standing there I seemed to be like a speck of dust in comparison to these huge monuments. To get up to the caves we had to climb many steps.

On the way we were harassed by young boys looking for money. I knew that it was not helpful to give but the innocence and pleading in the boys faces made it extremely difficult to refuse them. I was also aware that they were very adept at playing with my guilt feelings. I am sure they could read body language and knew exactly whom they should approach. I had been told on many occasions that to give in these situations only kept these young boys in bondage. It was difficult to believe this when you came face to face with them. "My name is Michael, remember me." This plea was incessant. In the end I relented. I moved along up the steps and to my horror I saw a man come around a corner and the boy had to hand over what he had. Lesson learned!

For those who could not make the walk, special chairs were adapted. There were two shafts on the front and on the back and two young fellows carried the incumbent up the hill.

We stayed in a local town called Aurangabad for the night and relaxed. We returned to Sadhana the following day. A driver was hired to take us there and back. It was like a scene from A Passage to India. The road trip was hair raising. I, who feared flying had to contend with passing vehicles on corners, or being uncomfortably close to cliff edges. "Right," said Kate who was almost silent for the entire car journey, "another angel on the bonnet!" We spent a few quiet days before returning home absorbing the experience. This time together as friends was a lifetime experience. Something neither of us would ever forget.

We returned home and were immediately separated and involved in our individual lives. I went over to visit Marie to see how she was. I brought her a gift but it only reminded her of her loss. Years later she spoke of this time. She said she resented me for going ahead to India. I explained to her that her biggest fear was not her friends but her fear around abandonment. How was she to survive if they turned against her? She said she knew all of this in her head but couldn't as yet, at eighty-two years of age, put it into practice. "Liz," she said, "do you ever think I will be able to move through this?" Only she could answer that one. Who was telling her that she shouldn't risk the trip? It had nothing to do with the people outside of her, but more the influences inside her mind.

Who is living in you? If you reflect you will notice that there isn't a gesture, a thought, an attitude or a belief that isn't coming from someone else. It's pretty painful when you recognise all the people who reside inside you, controlling your life.

*We will always be challenged
to be greater than we think
we are and life will present us
with the challenges to help
us move forward*

CHAPTER 22

Awareness Teaching

'There is but one cause of human failure and that is man's lack of faith in his true self'

William James

FRANCIS was relentless in his encouragement of my facilitating awareness seminars. He could see my passion not only for understanding awareness but my dogged pursuit of bringing it into daily living. Each day I reflected on my interactions with life, praying to see reality minus my inner programming. Anthony spoke of blindness. If you are blind, then how can you see? Is what you are now seeing, your programme or somebody else's? It was easy enough to identify what kept me stuck, what wasn't easy was taking courage and confronting whatever issue scared me. I always had a difficulty in standing up to people who never liked their authority being questioned. Insecure people easily resort to shouting at you, or finding passive aggressive ways to sabotage you. The course at Sadhana did help greatly. I was moving in the right direction. We will always be challenged to be greater than we think we are and life will present us with the challenges to help us move forward. Our problem is in trying to avoid the challenge not understanding the gift within it.

My main drawback to giving the seminars was my lack of training. I had the experience of awareness but not a degree or diploma in either Theology or Philosophy. That piece of paper is important in the minds of people. In today's world there is an ever increasing demand to have a certificate. Does that certificate really equip you for teaching? Not really: you also need experience. Though I know now there is nothing like life experience, my limiting thoughts played havoc with my ability to rustle up the courage to go out and teach. I kept attracting people to me who would question why Francis ever thought I was good enough to teach awareness. A few disparaging remarks here and there were not helpful to my self-esteem and I had to dig deep to find the source of my disquiet. On one occasion I was asked, "What qualifications do you have to do this, and might I add did you ever go for spiritual direction? What makes you think you are good enough?"

What they were really voicing was my own belief in myself. Nothing they said was any different from what I thought about myself. It made me look deeper as to why I would wish to share my experience. Francis saw it differently. He knew I was authentic. I had come through the toughest challenges and all of it only possible because of awareness. It was I who had huge misgivings about this. For me, I was only interested in the improvements in myself and the benefits for my family. Why could I not just enjoy this and continue my own learning, without the extra burden of teaching it and having to put myself at risk of ridicule?

I had two months to think about this and with the help of my daughters I created a brochure. My first talk was in Marino Institute in Dublin. Some friends came, as well as newcomers and once I got over the initial nervousness I was comfortable. Trying to find a way to teach from my own experience was difficult. It is much easier to quote people who have gone before. Showing people where awareness can be found in ordinary day to day living, made it seem to some as if I was saying I had made it. I knew that in no way I had. I had made genuine improvements but I was not claiming enlightenment.

I continued giving workshops at weekends while teaching during the week and giving meditation courses at night. Sometimes to groups of twenty, other times to four! It didn't matter so long as we all gained. People came for various reasons; one lady came to see if she could she get her daughter to come. She wanted to find out what it was all about. Another came because she had been given a gift of the course by her husband. He wanted her to change. Needless to say they were not in a frame of mind to accept what I was saying.

Initially I based it solely on Anthony's book, Awareness. I didn't appreciate my own experiences at the time. As time went by it became more my own. That needed to happen because we all need to evolve in our own way. We couldn't be dependent solely on his experience. Making the most of our own particular circumstances and our own experiences and our reactions to them became the objective. By the time I had given a few courses and had adjusted my way of delivering the course, I had undergone many changes personally. My confidence grew in what I was seeing and how I was interpreting it. What became the greatest gift was my understanding of what Anthony actually said. He said that we would change through understanding. That seeing is the most arduous thing you will ever do. It demands that you open your mind to challenge the thoughts and beliefs that have been your government.

I am a rescuer in recovery. There must be a twelve step programme for the likes of me! Rescuers have a favourite feeling and that is guilt. They somehow feel responsible for the happiness of the Universe. They seek out people in unawareness to help because it feeds their need to care and be seen as loving caring people. They feel an abundance of guilt over the minutia of incidents. My inability to state my intentions clearly, or to set in place priorities because I was guilt-ridden, was beyond explanation. So much talent is somewhere out there in the ether because it is not possible for it to be used properly because of guilt. Rescuers suffer from this more than most. Find out what is your controlling emotion. Understand it and discern where it no longer serves you.

There is a need within us to look for the dramatic, for enlightenment to come with lots of fanfare. When our lives are already bogged down in the ordinary it seems really good to have our transformation happen in a glamorous way. To some, that is what actually happens but for most of us it is a daily dropping off, a subtraction of ideas and beliefs, that frees us. That slow change was helpful to my family. A dramatic knowing would have drastically changed all our lives and none of us were ready for that.

Funny thing, I spent my life trying to change the people closest to me and found that it was as I changed, they changed. It happened, not by screaming and shouting but by seeing my part in my own difficulties and finding a new way to communicate.

Understanding and insight on their own are thoughts. Thoughts that are true insights need action. They will only remain as ideas in the head if not followed through. It was the following through that was essential for me and which brought about the greatest change.

CHAPTER 23

The Birth of Chetana

**'Courage is not the absence of fear,
but rather the judgement that something
else is more important than fear'**

Ambrose Redmoon

S ADHANA a way to God, Chetana God's way to us.

My own belief about myself that I was not good enough to teach Awareness continued to present itself on many occasions. Only when I gave the belief energy, could it control me. One evening Francis asked if I would be prepared to join him as facilitator in a December workshop in Dublin. I hesitated because groups were used to him coming to Ireland on his own and I knew there might be trouble ahead, especially as he was seen as the Indian Guru. He was aware of Anthony de Mello's dream of bringing this work into the ordinary, everyday life and what better way to do that but through someone who had walked the walk, who was rearing a family on her own, post separation and through awareness. This would be an opportunity of combining a male and female approach.

I continued to have serious doubts about my ability to present my understanding of awareness alongside Francis's vision for the continuation of Anthony's work. Let's face it, Francis was the Director of Sadhana for fourteen years. He had a Doctoral degree in Clinical Psychology and had lectured students at university level. I had a B.A. degree and a Diploma in Primary Teaching. I was a mother of four children. There was an imbalance in how people would perceive my role and his. Did I really want this? Would I have been better off doing as I had been doing up until then, giving courses to small groups of people who valued what I was teaching? Was I setting myself up for failure? What I didn't see was the fact that I had lived through very difficult circumstances and had managed it through my own interior work on awareness. Experience is vital in teaching awareness. It is not born out of the clouds or on an ideology that is unsustainable. It is practical.

It was a reality that the usual participants would have a difficulty. I had already faced accusations of "who do you think you are to do this and what qualifies you to teach?" My answer "Life experience of awareness". I was also aware that the opportunity just might not come again. His style of teaching was different and in the minds of the participants he had more authority than I had to speak on Awareness.

The first workshops did bring the response I expected and some participants went to Francis and asked that he facilitate the seminars on his own. My presence was pushing too many buttons. What I had to deal with was the effect of this response on me.

Francis's work centred on who we are and that lost connection to our Divine selves. His work was based on the process of Divinisation. Listening to him helped people experience something greater than self. My work brought us back to the present and had the effect of bringing us down to earth with a bang. The search for inner freedom begins with self and being human we all desire something outside of ourselves to make life better. It is only when we are brought to our knees that we stop and take stock of our lives. When we are sick of our sickness! I was no different. I would have loved an easier way out, some angel to magic the pain away. Some angel to take my thoughts and beliefs and transform them! Some spirit to do the actions for me, to face the challenges. It could never happen that way. God, the Universe, Spirit, whatever it means to you will not do one thing for you that you are capable of doing for yourself. That is your journey into freedom. Your ownership of your journey into happiness!

I thought of it this way. If I was constantly creating debt and someone came along and paid all of the debts for me on a regular basis, I would just continue the same pattern. It is the same with our thoughts and our beliefs. Unless we take a good look at them and sort the chaff from the wheat we will continue creating difficulty regardless.

Francis knew the value in how I approached awareness. He wanted to continue with Anthony de Mello's dream of bringing this to all people and understood that I had a vital role to play in this. The balance of having someone who had lived in a religious community and someone who had lived an ordinary life was good. He knew that I had walked the walk and now he wanted me to talk the talk. Awareness is not helpful at mind level as it becomes thought provoking without the necessary advantage of transformation. There cannot be change in this life unless you have a change of mind and a change of mind can mean a change of direction. Someone may be upset at your change and many were at mine. Yet, is it not selfish to demand that you remain unhappy, that you remain stuck, and that you remain a doormat, just to please another? He was looking to show people that awareness is something for all. Being aware is not confined to any group or individual. It is a way of being. A process by which you observe yourself in relation to life! It doesn't mean that you are so engrossed in observing yourself that you block out everything else going on around you. It is the art of being in tune with what is going on within you while at the same time being fully involved in life. Only you know your thoughts, your feelings and your reactions to coming in contact with reality. There is no one that can do this for you.

Initially the fight between my intellect and my emotional intelligence was intense. My intellect was developed and couldn't cope with my undeveloped emotional state. To admit, that although you are an adult you are operating emotionally at a child's level, is crippling. Who in their right mind really wants to face that unless you have to? Being comfortable exploring the mind is a recent phenomenon in Ireland. The fear that anyone would think you were cracking up had a debilitating effect. Shame was an important factor. When I see me as an adult, being brow beaten by a school principal because I dared to question something that needed questioning, when I see me blubbering like a child because she folded her arms and intimidated me, I see the truth of my undeveloped emotional state. I am acquainted with my own demons. I was terrified of voicing what I actually thought, giving an alternate opinion and standing my ground. I found it very difficult to receive any help but would be on red alert to give help. Receiving help in my mind meant that I was deficient in some way. If I did receive even the slightest offer of assistance the sense of obligation to repay propelled me to do something immediately. I would be so grateful for help yet at the same time I had that feeling of indebtedness linked to an abiding feeling of guilt. Being indebted to anyone made me feel uncomfortable, as if I were being controlled. Giving and receiving is a lifelong lesson. You need to be a mature adult to be able to give unconditionally. I only seemed to see what someone was doing for me while being blissfully unaware that giving and taking works both ways. The giver and taker both benefit. The giver is in the happy position to be able to give, and can choose to give if that is what they wish to do, but the receiver also has choices - do I or don't I receive? Sometimes you may be aware that there is massive payback expected and so refuse the gift. The payback might not be financial but emotional, "After all I did for you!" Sometimes you feel uncomfortable refusing. It is as if you are an ungrateful wench. There were times I did and dealing with the huff was not easy. Once I saw the huff I knew I made the correct decision. There was an expectation in the giving. There are times when moving out of a role can be unsettling for people who have been used to the old you.

In the unravelling of my part in the creation of distance in relationships I could see where and when it began in my marriage. I know now that when my husband said clearly before we married that he didn't feel ready for the responsibility of a more permanent relationship, I did not listen. I could not see how someone so kind and loving could ever have a difficulty. I was too young to realise what pressure can do to a relationship. Being over responsible, I was in no position to see it from his point of view. In later years, I could see that my refusal to go out to teach and use my qualifications would have had consequences. We were both at either end of the argument. I wanted to be at home with our children and he, being fearful of being the sole provider when I initially decided to resign from teaching, wanted me to continue. I felt that I had an opportunity to stay at home, and I don't regret that decision, but it made me vulnerable too. Staying at home also had consequences for me. I found it difficult to be dependent. I needed to justify my decision and went into overdrive being the good housewife. I no longer felt equal in the relationship. When I went back to teaching I had not worked enough years cumulatively to provide me with a decent pension.

Guilt from that decision to stay at home left me in the shadows. Feeling I had disappointed him and had not lived up to his expectations was the beginning of my downfall. My self-esteem lowered. I slowly but surely became invisible. My not feeling equal in the relationship insidiously fed the discord for years until something had to give. Unexplored resentments fester. We never did discuss these problems together nor did we discuss them in a safe environment where both of us could be heard. Our fears surrounding counselling were too many and varied. Counselling would have been an acknowledgement that there was something amiss. It was at this point of desperation that I opened my eyes through my own internal investigation. It was as a result of this experience that I knew that awareness based on intellect was totally useless, that becoming a mystic was less important to this world than becoming aware. The knock on effect of my own progress benefited my children. That was my total priority. The fear of not bringing everyone with me on this journey was intense yet the fear of passing on my way of dealing with life and those consequences, pushed me deeper and deeper into my investigation of self.

As time went on I understood that psychology on its own

could only take me a certain distance and that religion wasn't my answer either. What I was searching for was total freedom and religion as I experienced it was keeping me infantile. My God was a controlling, angry father, waiting for me to make mistakes so that I could be heavily punished. I will not dispute that religion held the space for me until I came to a state where I could finally step forward to experience a direct contact with the Divine. Religion was my middle man for years. Now I needed to go straight to Source.

I needed to go beyond the mind, beyond religion to a world within me, and only I could take that step. There was no formula to do this and neither was there a guarantee that I would ever experience it. I had this sense of knowing that in chiselling away at what wasn't true I might have some hope of finding truth.

In all my male relationships I felt inferior. Something within me prevented me from assuming my right to speak openly and freely. Working with Francis I saw that I was still suffering. If I am to look at this pragmatically I can see clearly why people would choose to listen to Francis. To them, I was watering down the message. Many people felt that because Francis was in personal contact with Anthony that somehow or other he was Anthony, though Francis would be the first to admit that there were many people living and working with Anthony who did not appear greatly affected by his work. My sense of inequality was some mental mountain for me to climb.

There was no escaping this challenge. The first to highlight that there was a danger was my mother. When she spotted a weakness she felt obliged to let me know her discovery.

I happened to bring down a brochure that I thought was really good and a very important step forward. She took it in her hand and her face took on 'that look'. It is a look that said I have discovered the one thing you do not want to hear. "Hmmm. Where do you feature on this brochure? This is all about Francis. I thought you would have had more sense than to go back down that road. This has no mention of you, your last brochure was yours on your own. A step back if ever there was one," she declared. I came out reeling at first but laughed later. She was right. Not easily digested but how was I to rectify this one?

Central to my growth was the challenge surrounding my divorce. This legal hassle had been going on for years. I learned one truth and that was that no one could tell me what to do, or what was in the best interests for me or the children. They could advise but ultimately we were the ones to live with the consequences. If I had moved on advice given to me without discernment on my part, I would have been in a more vulnerable state. Not to take responsibility for my decisions would have kept me in blame prison. Any move I made I had to make it in the full knowledge that this was my choosing. Ultimately I came to a point where there was no choice, there was only a way forward. Once I came to see the way forward I had to go. It was like cutting a way through a dense forest. Moving from familiar to unfamiliar, from known to unknown is a problem for most of us.

Scott Peck spoke of this in his book, The Road Less Travelled. What I was taking from awareness was full responsibility for the part of my life that I was responsible for. I did what I needed to do and then took a breathing space to allow the consequences of that decision to take hold. What I noticed was that once I moved and waited, the next move was shown to me. I had learned to be patient and not to push the river. Though I thought I was in deep trouble, I actually wasn't. I never felt more supported than at that time. It was as if in observing all that was going on around me I was much more aware of unseen forces helping me out.

I would ask a question and an answer would appear in a book, on a bill board or through something a person would say. The feeling was of being fully alive, aware of being helped in ways I had not ever thought of. I never felt on my own. Though I was alone, I was not lonely. From needing people's approval to becoming independent was a wonderful transition. Sometimes the going got very tough and I reached out to friends but no one was there. No matter how many times I phoned there was no reply. The penny dropped that this was time to stay still, trust, and go through the eye of the needle. Even if it meant crying for the day, the tears eventually dried and I emerged a better person. Each day I surrendered to a truth I did not fully understand but knew was available to me. Not my will but thine be done and I trusted those moments. I was cutting the umbilical cord of dependency. Ultimately I would have to let go of the beliefs I had about my known God. The image of God created by man.

This is how I see it now. How I see it now is this way. The connection I had with my image of God was one of father/daughter. All images were created by my understanding. The more I cleared my way of thinking the more I could see there is no separation between me and God, as we are all one. My old images had to go and I feared that. I waited for the punishment and found contentment.

This is what Francis was seeing in me when he asked me to join him and teach under the name Chetana - God's Way to Us. Sadhana was our way to God. I continued to have my reservations about teaching. I could see that some people were not ready for this joint venture. On the other hand, there were many who said, "I do not know how this works but it does. You are coming from two different worlds." My world was earthed and challenging for people who would have preferred a more dramatic spiritual experience.

Anything that looks simple you can be guaranteed has taken time and patience. When some participants came they had an idea of what awareness was all about. They had expectations and I had mine. They did not always a match. People have to want what you have to give. I also needed to find out what they wanted and see if I could I meet that need. What kept me on track were the numerous women who were open to listening. As one lady put it to me when we were giving a retreat in Sligo, "Have you been secretly listening to me in my kitchen, your story is very close to mine? Is it possible for me to change?" "This freedom is available to us all," I replied. It was comments like these that kept me seeing the usefulness of my work, that there were people out there happy to listen. I know I made many mistakes in my delivery. By relying totally on personal examples sometimes gave the impression that I was saying I had made it. I haven't, I just happen to be further on than I used to be. My intention was to show that if it is possible for me, then it is possible for you.

With the completion of our first Chetana retreat in The Royal Marine Hotel in Dún Laoghaire, Francis felt that I was ready to teach at Sadhana Institute in India. Our first Chetana retreat in India was in March 2003. The majority of participants were women and men in leadership positions in the Church. It was for one week. Four sessions each day! We worked for the first four days on personal observation of beliefs, habits, and relationships. On the last day we showed how chiselling away at what creates separation within our personal relationships, could help us see what creates separation between us and our Divinity - Our minds! Even if you are not looking for a spiritual experience but a direction as to how to empty your mind of what is controlling you, awareness of how you relate to people and life, it is essential. It was received well and I returned in June to give another retreat. In the meantime, I was teaching in the school. I was fortunate in that the Chairperson of the Board of Management and P.J my Principal agreed to let me go. He could see how this work was positively impacting on the children in the school.

My position in the school was in Learning Support and Special Education. This gave me the opportunity to work with the children individually or in small groups. This was also the time of the school garden. Various organisations donated plants, soil, and their time. When I look at the age group that dug out rocks in those initial stages I am in awe. They were so little and the work was demanding. They loved it because it was practical and hands on.

Some teachers brought their classes out in summer time and they sat and read stories. We had a sensory, herb, fruit, vegetable and flower garden. A very kind and knowledgeable lady helped me build a willow tunnel. As many children as was possible were involved in the planting. We won prizes in numerous competitions which also helped towards the funding of the project. Winning to me was not as important as the daily joy the garden gave to the children. It was there I heard their stories. I can see myself working away on bended knee with a little one beside me. The fact I was not directly looking at him or her gave them the space to let me know what was happening in their lives. Though it was not necessary for me to do anything, my being able to listen was vital. We all need that and children are no exception.

The more seminars I facilitated the more insight I gained from my own interior self. What we focus our attention on grows and my reflections on my own life helped me shape my talks. Chetana was truly God's way to me. The more I taught Awareness the more I loved the work. It was gathering momentum. I loved teaching in the school and especially working with the children yet in the back of my mind I was wondering if I worked with parents could I make more headway. An Inspector came to the school on a whole school inspection and asked me what I did to make such changes in the school environment. I told her I worked on me. The more I changed the more change happened. She wasn't happy with the answer. She said, "Teachers will look for ways to change the children not ways to change themselves. This is not something you can package easily." I knew that.

A decision had to be made. Where did I wish to be, in the school or out giving seminars? If this was to work, I had to quit the day job. How much did I want Chetana? Enough to give up a pensionable day job! The signs were that if I was free to work then it would take off. I needed more time to write and reflect. It was too late in the year to apply for sabbatical leave. I decided to resign, to take that brave step and jump off the cliff. Divorce proceedings were in full swing and a date had been set for October. I knew that I would be paid until the end of August and perhaps this would be sufficient time to centre myself on the work. I trusted with all my heart that a way would be found to support us and it was, but I wonder at times at my decision. It was not practical, but then major decisions sometimes are not practical.

I had a trip to India coming up the following August. I didn't have enough time previously to really explore India. For the most part I landed in Bombay and a jeep would take me to Sadhana. I would give the talks and head home. Francis asked if I would like to go on a pilgrimage to Varanasi... and I accepted.

How did I feel about leaving teaching? I felt released until the final day when I saw little Glenn walk down the corridor of the school. He had his arms outstretched. "You know what these are for Miss?" he said. "They are for you; I'll miss ya." In that moment I fully realised how much I would miss them too.

We see people not as they are but as we are. We look through our lens of perception and our lens is based on our experience. No one likes to discover that they are operating at the emotional level of a teenager. I made that discovery.

Many of the people I had already met during the retreats, so I was not a total foreigner to them. It was lovely meeting them in their own surroundings. It gave me greater insight into how difficult the message we were teaching was for them

CHAPTER 24

The Pilgrimage

'Most people would rather be certain they're miserable than risk being happy'

Robert Anthony

I WAS overjoyed at the prospect of seeing some more of India. On my mother's side there is a strong connection with India. In 1787 the Governor of Madras's daughter, Margery, married a McVeagh of Drewstown, Co. Meath. This house is situated about two miles from my own childhood home. My great grandmother was Emily McVeagh who was a direct descendent and lived in Drewstown. Her brother George married Maude Benson, whose father was a lieutenant general in the Madras Regiment. In Bangalore there is a road called Benson Road. It was an extraordinary coincidence that I, too, should also have a passage to India.

The trip to India was planned for August and at the same time Grace was planning to leave for Japan. She hadn't any date set and I was uneasy at the prospect of her leaving before my return. When nothing final was happening I decided to go ahead with my pilgrimage.

I arrived at Sadhana and rested for a few days. Edwina who was administrator welcomed me with open arms.

Francis had the itinerary and I trusted that he knew the best places to visit. I had been so busy prior to the journey that I did absolutely no research. There was accommodation at every stop of the way. This is the joy of belonging to a religious community. They have beautiful centres throughout the countryside. It may have been a bit unusual that we journey together, however, I was extended the best of hospitality. Many of the people I had already met during the retreats, so I was not a total foreigner to them. It was lovely meeting them in their own surroundings. It gave me greater insight into how difficult the message we were teaching was for them. In previous years Anthony tended to discourage someone from coming to Sadhana on their own to attend a course. To be able to make personal changes you needed some support but even more after you begin to see and changes begin to happen. Seeing many of the nuns I realised this truth very quickly. It is easy to be full of enthusiasm for ideas when surrounded by people who understand where you are coming from, but not so easy in a closed minded sorority.

Edwina accompanied us to Dadar station in Bombay. On my first trip to India, Francis told me that I could go to Dadar and get a train to Lonavla. "Get a taxi from the airport to the station," he said. "It is very convenient!" I took one look at the place and knew I would have been overwhelmed. I had lived such a sheltered life, with little experience of life and Dadar was beyond explanation. I couldn't breathe at first. I had never experienced as many people and as much activity in a confined space before. I do know that some adventurous people do this all the time and they are quite fearless. I was not one of them. I was still very much aware that I had a young child at home and recklessness was not one of my traits. The train had thirty-two carriages. Francis was familiar with the system and was able to locate our carriage. We had a carriage where you could sleep. This initial journey was for twenty-four hours. I was so exhausted I think I slept for at least sixteen of them. The carriage was cramped and there were four bunks. Every so often some vendors went around announcing items for sale. They also had menus. We ordered, they phoned the order in to the next station and when the train stopped, we got our order. It was freshly cooked and delicious.

Eventually we arrived at our first destination, Benares also known as Varanasi. It is the spiritual capital of India. After attaining enlightenment in Bodh Gaya, Buddha came to Sarnath some thirteen kilometres outside Varanasi, and preached his first sermon in the Deer Park in 528 BC. Varanasi is a major centre for pilgrimages. It's known worldwide for its many ghats: stone steps leading down to the Ganges River where pilgrims perform ritual ablutions and Hindus cremate their dead.

We met up with a friend and he walked with us through the tiny streets. All forms of living were drawn together in an amazing web. On the one hand you had street trading, shops, ashrams, Hindu ceremonies, on the other you had simple living. An old man ironed clothes with an iron that I remember in museums, the back of it opened to allow him place hot coals inside. In what looked no more than a tea chest turned sideways he operated his business. Beside him a lady who lived under a tarpaulin washed her little child. The naked little fellow was jumping up and down. He did not like the experience of a pot of water being thrown over his head, or his teeth being washed but she continued regardless. We strolled towards the Ghats. Hundreds of people bathed quite naturally. Others got into boats and placed small candles into wax saucer like containers and placed them on the river. We got into one of the boats and I bought some candles and lit one for each of my children and placed them in the water as we quietly sailed down the river. I quietly prayed for their happiness.

We continued along the river and we noticed a sign for Varanasi silks. The city is famous for its muslin and silk fabrics as well as perfumes and sculptures. I mentioned to Francis that I would like to see what they had for sale. It was a feast of silk. I bought some bed covers for my children. We spoke to the owners for a while. In the middle of the conversation the name Lahiri Mahasaya, a famous Indian Guru emerged. I had heard some talk of him and was interested in hearing more. Lahiri was known for Kriya Yoga. This man said that his home was nearby and he would ask the boatman to take us to his ashram. Though Lahiri was long dead, his descendants were still living.

We sailed our way downstream and arrived at our destination. It did not take long to find the house. Francis was able to explain why we were there and we were ushered into a small room. A picture of Lahiri was on the wall in front of me. None of us felt like speaking. A young man entered. He explained in Hindi that he had been meditating and to excuse him as he was still in a deepened state. He looked at me for some moments. I got the impression he was uncomfortable. He spoke then only to Francis. He appeared to have the impression that he had reached Enlightenment. I observed him as he spoke. He clearly had a problem with women, perhaps only Western women. He didn't behave any differently to the Indian ladies present so there were no preferences. We were all treated somewhat the same. Through his conversations with Francis we discovered that he was only minding the place. The direct descendant was in America teaching.

I was glad to have visited and to have learned more. What I loved about Lahiri's story was that he was unusual among Indian Gurus in that he was married with a family. He worked as an accountant for the Military Engineering Department of the British Indian government. He lived an ordinary life and it was only after he retired that he devoted his life to Kriya Yoga. Lahiri insisted in his teachings that if you are earning an honest living, and practicing honestly there was no need to alter your external life in order to become aware of connection to all there is. He encouraged people to meditate and to clear their minds of dogma in order to have direct contact with Divine Presence. I liked this. We were coming back to the same teaching in that awareness is there for everyone. There is no discrimination. We didn't have to leave our ordinary jobs in order to experience Divine presence in our lives.

We got back into our row boat and sailed back. We could not get back on land for some time because the bulls had decided to bathe and there was no way of reaching the steps. They ambled their way up the steps. When they finished they made their way through the streets.

We climbed up the steps and I noticed some activity to my right. I climbed further up and realised to my horror it was a funeral pyre. As is common in India a young guy came forward to explain what was happening. I could see that the body was beautifully wrapped in a sari and she was brought to the Ganges for immersion in the holy waters. Then she was carried and placed on top of the pyre. I noticed there were only men present and was told that women are emotional and this could delay the soul's journey. A holy man walked around the pyre blessing it before it was lit. I never ever would have believed that I could witness this. There were times I saw it on television and would immediately switch stations, but here it was different. There was a sense of sacredness that cannot be communicated on television.

We moved along to have lunch in an Ashram run by some Catholic nuns. It was one of the sisters' birthdays and a veritable feast was laid out for her. We sat on the floor in a circle as dish after dish was served. It was delicious.

I could not leave Varanasi without visiting Sarnath. Sarnath is the site where

Buddha gave his first sermon. I wanted to quietly inhale the place and left Francis to be with his friend who had accompanied us for the day. I was strolling along at my own pace when an elderly holy man approached. His eyes were piercingly kind. There was an aura of peace about him. I welcomed his guidance. Though I hadn't the language he brought me to the most sacred places. I wondered later if it was the actual place or this beautiful being's presence that touched me. Without direct communication we communicated. I left him to join Francis and his friend. I looked around to say goodbye and he was gone. Nowhere was he in sight. It was as if he just evaporated.

Our next stop on our journey was Agra. We met up with Joe, a priest who had recently attended Sadhana. He welcomed me warmly. He was our tour guide for the two days and his courteousness and kindness stays with me.

The Taj Mahal is everything people say it is. Built by the Mughal Emperor Shah Jahan in memory of his third wife Mumtaz Jahan, walking through the Great Gate is like walking into another world. When people think of India generally their first thoughts are often about the poverty of the country. Alongside it is also such grandeur and splendour. India has its extremes and it is not possible for us to comprehend any of it in a short visit.

Down the centre of the garden leading up to the mausoleum is a rectangular water way. On either side are raised walkways. The reflection of the Taj Mahal is to be seen in the water. Seeing the intricate inlaid design for the first time makes you wonder at our structures today. What have we built in this century that can compare to this magnificence? As tired as I was with the heat of the sun I wanted to take in as much as possible on my visit.

Onwards by train to Delhi! I loved sitting in the trains, looking out at scenery and people. Saris and flowers, trucks and buildings all creating a tapestry of colour. We arrived in Delhi and it was hot and humid. We got to our accommodation. This time we did not know any of the people present in this men's community. Our contact was away. It was the first place that I felt uncomfortable and unwelcome. I have no problem with silence, in fact I welcome it, but this was different. One silent meal was enough for me. We couldn't avoid this community of priests. There was one large table with a circular piece in the centre. If you needed anything like pepper and salt you could spin it around to where you were sitting. I hadn't seen one like this before.

It wasn't just the elective silence that got me but an air of superiority, perhaps a sense of intellectualism that was off-putting. I knew we would only be spending a day there and was I grateful for the rest at least. I mentioned to Francis that I would not be attending the evening meal! I was quite content to eat a banana and some biscuits. I was happy to be in my own company.

Delhi alone could take a few weeks to explore. We had an agenda and kept things simple by keeping to it. The house where Gandhi spent the last days of his life before being assassinated was our first stop. They have even marked the spot where he died. This is a fascinating place to visit. Not only do you get the life of Gandhi but there is also an arcade where you can either read or follow the history of India through photos and drawings. You would need a full day to take it in.

We moved to Humayun's tomb which is said to be the inspiration for the Taj Mahal. In Irish terms it is like the difference between Slieve na Caillighe and Newgrange. Slieve allows you a quieter experience. If I were to do it again I would go to Humayun's tomb first and learn about Mughal architecture and then see how it influenced the Taj.

Then we visited the Lotus Temple! This is the Baha'i House of Worship. The Baha'i faith is one of the youngest of world religions. The Temple took ten years to build and it is probably one of the most complicated constructions in the world. It is truly in the shape of a lotus. They have a system where you and maybe thousands of others, hand up your shoes and then queue for a long time to get in. It is worth the wait as you sit there surrounded by its beauty and peace. Delhi in less humid weather is a must.

How quickly the time passed! The person who began the journey was not the person at the end of it. We boarded Rajdhani Express, a beautiful high speed train. This was very classy and we made our way back to Bombay. I was happy to reach Sadhana and Edwina. She extended her usual warm welcome and we spent hours recounting the tales, sitting in that lovely room upstairs, drinking Bailey's cream liquor and eating spiced toasted nuts. Gladys, a young nun who joined the convent when she was fifteen years old, was also present. She had attended all of our Chetana retreats and it was wonderful to relax with her before making the journey home.

When home I had to face the sadness of Grace's pending departure to Japan. Part of me shut down and did not want to either think or talk about it. We had spent so much time together that this separation was certain to be painful. Japan was alien to me and though there was one part of me that wished it would not happen, another part knew that Grace was moving into her own life and it would be pure selfishness on my part to demand that she stay. I dreaded the thought that she be given a date when I was away. Something in my gut said go on your journey, that all is well.

It was the beginning of the end of an era and the letting go was not easy. You invest so much time and energy in your family but you quickly realise that you do not own them or their hearts. This is how it is meant to be. They, too, had to find themselves. Grace had to find her way. I did not want her to be a mini me but in letting her go I had to practise what I preached.

September 23rd saw us all at the airport. She was finally heading to Tokyo. I would never have imagined that within two years three of my children would be living the other side of the world. A mass exodus. I coped by blocking how I actually felt. I had this image that they would live in Ireland and travel the world for the odd adventure. I looked forward to the day they would be independent of me and I could be involved in their lives as adults. I had grown accustomed to meeting the girls for coffee and a chat.

This was the beginning of the shattering of that dream. I questioned my own travels. Did I sow the seed for this? To make it easier for both of us she stayed with Michelle the week before departure. I see her being brave and sad as she looked out the window of Michelle's house before we headed to the airport. She wasn't fully sure if she was being met at Narita airport and this caused me some anxious moments. She knew what she was doing and I didn't want to pressure her. I stood at the departure gates and hugged her, tears flooding down my face. I said, "You know I do not want you to go, but if you chose to stay because of me I would push you onto that plane. This is your life and you must live it and honour that." Watching my children go through those departure gates was extremely painful. They were so young.

Detachment, detachment, detachment Anthony would say is the answer. There is no attachment in love. My understanding of detachment was flawed. Did detachment mean you could no longer feel the deepest emotions, did it mean distancing from people, a shutting down of the heart. It is actually the opposite. Feel the depth of emotion but don't cling to it. Experience the beautiful and the sad feelings but let them pass. Don't cling to them. It was easy to be that way in relation to the children in the school as they had parents. Easy to see clearly when you are not emotionally engaged. Understanding what was going on allowed me to let the pain pass and bless her on her way.

There is a natural grieving process that must be acknowledged otherwise you are fooling yourself. Rearing children takes up so much of your life that the suddenness of their departure takes you unawares. The children had become my world especially since the separation. Awareness had come back to bite me. When I first became aware of my behaviour in relationships and how they impacted on my children, I moved as best I could into a new way of looking at life. Instead of constantly reacting to situations, I discerned more before I acted. I couldn't hide what was happening from them but whether I liked it or not I involved them. Separation is like a slow death and as I had been the one to instigate it, it appeared as if I did not go through pain. If you are the chooser, then you are meant to be in a better place to deal with it.

This isn't true. Each step you must go deeper within you and you begin to doubt your resources. Knowing you have changed you don't have the option of turning back. It is like climbing a ladder, you look back and see there are no steps to go down. Once you see you can never un-see. I had to let go of the attachment to my old dreams about my children and my marriage. To stay the way we were would have been to stay in the cocoon and ultimately would have led to resentment. What also emerged was the truth that no matter where my children lived they resided in my heart. Love is not duty, clinging, jealousy, demands, expectations, or guilt. Love cannot reside in a house filled with anger and resentment. There is freedom in living the truth. Letting go of old programmes is difficult. Seeing the blossoming of your children as they evolve is the reward.

No attachment was the message. We must evolve and move on from what has gone before. Even if Grace never left the country she would still have to psychologically make that journey into herself. If she clung to me or I to her neither of us could become who we were meant to be. Neither of us could be free, and neither could we have a good relationship. It is the way.

I understand now what Jesus was saying. You must leave your mother, father, brothers and sisters before you can enter the kingdom of God. He didn't mean deny them, or remove yourself physically. I had to let go my attachment to my children if they were to be free. They must be free to live their lives as they see fit.

CHAPTER 25

The Final Curtain

'Focus your attention on your intention'

Anon

I KEEP observing at every turn that reality is not the problem. Our reaction to reality, our perception of reality is what causes stress. Each of us responds in our own way. To some, challenge is invigorating, to another it is paralysing. On the outside to all intents and purposes I should have been stressed out of my tree. I had resigned from my teaching post, and was moving closer to my divorce. Grace had only gone to Japan three weeks previously and I missed her dreadfully.

Time after time, challenge after challenge came out of the woodwork to test my strength. I was being pushed way out of my comfort zone. Get the divorce, get on with my life, but a mistake now would have had long term consequences not just for me but also for the children. Any time I felt I was being unreasonable I would receive information of one kind or another to show me that nothing had changed and every attempt to get the upper hand was in place. What was also interesting was how I felt outside of it all, looking in. An onlooker, a witness to what was happening! Every day I went through the same ritual of prayer to guide me. I know that all of us can get caught up in anger and a sense of injustice. I prayed for God's will, Universal Wisdom in this.

I walked around Leopardstown Racecourse and sat under my favourite tree yet again asking to be shown the next step. No matter what happened I waited until the confusion had eased and a way found. When I took action I blessed it and waited until the next challenge and started the whole process all over again. This way I felt I did not act from vindictiveness but was guided through these times. My friend in all of these matters was Rose, my solicitor. She didn't push me one way or another and greatly respected my views.

When I asked her to let go of my first Barrister in the divorce proceedings because I knew that he did not have the emotional strength to deal with the opposition she said, "Liz, what am I going to say to him?" I told her that too much was at stake for me to get involved with his feelings. Though he was a perfect gentleman this would be me returning to my old pattern of not wishing to hurt his feelings while I got shafted.

I could see from our previous foray into the Law Library that he was no match for this lady Barrister. I could see it as he scuttled away from her. Each time he went to the court to get some information for our case he came back not with the information but with more demands. Rose got me a new barrister. She knew what I was about and what was needed. When Una arrived on the scene everything changed. Interesting that in the legal separation I went from female barrister to a male to get heard, but now, this was in reverse. I had no specific attachment to anyone other than someone who could do the job well. Una had the skills of a forensic scientist and the coolness of a polo mint.

Eventually another chance at sorting it out in the Law Library! This time it was more realistic. I could hear the opposing Barrister shouting and threatening me but it had absolutely no effect. I could see that my barrister was not in the least fazed by her behaviour. "Wait until I get her in the stand!" and so it went on. This time I was not going to be intimidated. We came to a point where I was asked if I felt that agreement could be made. I asked if I could leave them for some moments and go out to the yard. I needed to pray that this was fair for all of us. I stayed out there for as long as I felt I needed before I went back and said I would sign.

Once I signed it, I left the building! Una and Rose brought me to a little café for a cup of coffee. They had major concerns for me because in their opinion I should not have left a pensionable job. I reassured them that all would be well and I hoped that my work with Francis and my own personal work would continue.

I thanked them and walked up the quays to get the car. I had little or no petrol in it. I saw that there was a garage on the opposite side of the quays and made my way there. It all seemed surreal. Did that just happen? Was this really the end of twenty-two years of marriage and nine years of painstakingly making our way towards this end? I stopped for petrol and to my amazement a huge poster billing was in front of me and on it were the words "Blue Moon". I felt my father-in-law was with me in spirit. Years previously when I was with Paddy McMahon for a spiritual reading he said "your father-in-law is here and he is humming Blue Moon. Every time I heard the song or saw the words I could feel his presence envelope me.

What was amazing was the synchronicity of numbers! I know problems began when our first child was born. It was then that I began to change my mind as to what path to follow. She was born on 17th October and I was 26 years old then. This final settlement was on 17th October and she was 26 years old and we were number 17 on the list. A numerologist or an astrologer would have had a field day around that!

When the documents were finally signed the judge looked at me and asked if I felt happy that there was no provision for me in the settlement. I knew that I had my teaching if I needed to return and replied, "Yes." I needed to be on my own for a short while to let go of the sadness around the expectations of our marriage but also accept fully the knowledge that what I had just completed was right for us all. So long as I continued to be over responsible, John could never become free. This too was his chance at freedom.

No one can give you a method for self-observation. It means to watch everything that is happening within you and around you as if it were happening to someone else. You do not personalise it, you look at it as if you have no connection to it. Emotions and judgements personalise!

*A date was set for leaving.
January 10th, 2004 the
anniversary of my father's death.
I wasn't going to forget that.
There had been so much
healing around him the
week before he died*

CHAPTER 26

Moving on

'Be the change you want to see'
Mahatma Gandhi

I CAME home and opened the front door. It was eerie. Like a death had happened. I knew that as long as we lived in that house, it would make it difficult for all of us as a family to move forward. Even those walls carried memories and associations. Every time they returned they would revert to being children. This had been our family home. It would be difficult for me to engage in a new life with that expectation.

I contacted many estate agents to see what they considered a fair price for the house. It was time to move on. As the only child now living in the house was Annie, where we moved to had more to do with what was best for her. Initially she was upset at leaving her familiar surroundings. Grace was in Japan and Paul and Michelle had left the family home and were shortly to leave the country so it wasn't easy for her. I asked her to trust me that I would find a place that would suit us both. Within three days I accepted an offer higher than all the estate agents had expected for the house. I knew I would have no problem selling as it was in a beautiful area, near shops, schools, and a magnificent park. The garden in the back was large and over the years I had spent hours developing it. I loved that garden but I could no longer give it the time it needed. I wasn't expecting the sale to be so quick.

A date was set for leaving. January 10th 2004 the anniversary of my father's death. I wasn't going to forget that. There had been so much healing around him the week before he died. I had sat with him in the hospital. We had many differences throughout the years. He looked cold and I pulled his cardigan up around him. He said, "You know, I never meant any harm though it might seem that way!" I said, "I now understand that. I see life differently. Are you ok Dad?" "I am now," he replied and smiled contentedly. That was the last time I saw him alive. I didn't need him to say sorry. Neither did he need me to forgive him. We had both moved through pain.

I had three months to find a home. In the meantime, I had to contend with solicitors. I was told that I would get a fair deal because of the expenditure around the divorce.

I wanted a house with no reminders. I went to numerous estate agents and followed properties on the internet. One day I walked into P. B. Gunne's estate agents in Dún Laoghaire. I told the girls that I did not want a house in my own area, too many memories, yet I had a feeling that they had my house. They had nothing on offer. Still the feeling persisted. It was getting scary. We had no place to live if this did not work out. I had given up my secure job. There was no way I would be given a loan and neither could I re-mortgage the house if the sale fell through. The only thing keeping us from the breadline was that some money came in from the car accident of three years earlier. It wasn't much but we could survive for another two months. We would have to wait until the house was sold and a smaller house bought until we were sorted. Having searched every district, I came to the realisation that not one place was as near shops, Annie's school or a park as beautiful as the one that was within walking distance from our house.

As I sat under a big tree in the park this insight came to me. I thought about my reasons for leaving. I wanted to run away from the familiar, from people who knew me and reminded me of the past. It was a fair enough point but it was crippling us. I decided there and then that my ego could and would be sacrificed. I put the details into the computer yet again and this time included my district. There it was! I went down to P. B. Gunne's and said that I would like to see this particular property. They looked at me doubtfully. I said I had had a change of mind and would just like to see it. We made an appointment for the next day and as I walked through the door I said, "This is my house." My initial instinct was correct. Now I had to go through hoops before I could come to this but I kept to the initial intention and it worked out. Throughout the experience I never lost sight of our priorities. I made an offer.

I met a friend and we had a coffee. I said that I would have to have a deposit of €7000 by the morning. She asked, "Where are you going to get it?" "Right now, I have no idea." By 5pm I had two offers of help. I knew it was a temporary loan and it would be given back when everything went through, but I was deeply grateful.

I spoke again to the solicitor who was very put out that I should even consider accepting an offer without first consulting him. He recommended that I wait until we had moved out.

I asked him, "Where are we to live in the meantime? Where is my child supposed to go? This house is exactly what we need and I feel in these matters it is I who makes that decision." He was not pleased. His pace at sorting out details was painstakingly slow and he got angry if I made enquiries.

I was given the 18th December as the date to sign the contracts. I needed one tenth of the value of the property. Kate my close friend, gave it to me willingly. You would think she was handing over a bar of chocolate. "It's only money," she said.

Then the solicitor told me that he would not prepare the contracts until after Christmas. Though he was in the office he did not have the time to sort out the documents. I got angry. "This lady is going to pull this house off the market if it is not finalised before Christmas, and you are blocking it. I will make you responsible if this happens." He was suddenly available. He had everything in place by the time I arrived. Then he produced his bill. He seemed to think that he was entitled to one and a half percent of the value of the property. The estate agents seemed to think likewise. I do not know where this sense of entitlement came from. I had to do so much of the work myself and follow things through, while in the meantime they were about to put their greedy hands into my pocket. As my father would put it, "I was under the impression I was paying you." That being so you are working for me not me for you.

I reminded the solicitor of my agreement with his junior solicitor. He said that he had since left and any agreement made unless in writing would not be honoured. I looked at him squarely and asked, "And exactly what is going to be left for me and Annie by the time you have finished with this?" "What do you mean?" "Neither house is old. Both were built around the same time. There is no problem with searching for titles. Everything is in order and as it should be. What gives you the right to charge this fee for so little work?" He took five thousand euro off the fee. Another bag of courage embodied!

We had our last Christmas in the house. Each one of us with our own memories! I could not think too deeply about it because I needed to be calm for Annie's sake. I began to pack the contents of the house. Kate gave me umpteen boxes and I catalogued everything. It came down to the larger furniture. The old couch needed to go to the tip head. I thought a charity shop might like some of the other furniture but was clearly told that no one wants old furniture today. We were down to two beds and the echo in the house was getting louder by the day. The attics were emptied and the house had a hollow sound. What were we to do with Annie's wardrobe? I had nowhere to put it. I pulled it out to the back garden and took an axe to it. I apologised to Annie that not even a charity shop would take her wardrobe. She took out her camera and took photos of me with a hatchet bludgeoning the old thing to pieces. We laughed until we pained.

When everything was more or less gone I got a phone call from the estate agent. He asked if a representative from the bank could come and inspect the property. This was one week from our supposed departure. That is where I almost crumbled. What if this man's loan was not accepted? We had an empty house and no money to get any more furniture. I had no job. This angered me so much because in my mind this estate agent should have had all of this in order. Not until the final day did we know if we were actually moving or not. The night before, I sat on Annie's bed!

"Mum, what are we going to do?" "I can panic or I can laugh," I replied. Then the two of us looked at each other and laughed. We made noises to emphasise just how empty the house was. Both of us slept soundly that night.

The new owner wanted possession on the exact date. I had a removals van waiting. Nothing could be done until he signed the final documents and paid the remainder of the money owed. Only then could I pay the owner of my house. The solicitor was out of reach. He neither texted nor phoned! I telephoned my friend Rose and asked if she could find any information for me. He did phone eventually and seemed extremely put out that I should contact him. We were on standby until five o clock that afternoon. I did not feel that I was being unreasonable. The removers were asking for more money as this was taking longer than usual. Paul came over and gave me a hug. This delay with the solicitor was like the final straw that broke the camel's back.

We had to lock our cat in my bedroom as she was scared witless. All hands were on deck as we moved the remainder of the stuff into my car. My young niece Rebecca, who was over from New Zealand, wrapped Felix in a blanket. I was afraid that she would run away. I needn't have bothered. She panicked under a duvet for nearly three months after the move. Once McNabb our dog saw that we were not leaving her behind she was very happy. There is very little distance between the two houses so we were able to walk her. Michelle and her fiancé James, Annie, Paul and Rebecca were masters at moving out. Rebecca took every box marked kitchen and locked herself in the kitchen. She sorted everything out beautifully. I had to get piano removers to move the piano. When they saw the eight steps up to the house they were saying prayers for me. A year later they were saying more prayers because I gave the piano to my daughter Michelle. It was like a boomerang as six months later she was sending it back to me because she was emigrating to Australia. Paul was heading to New Zealand and Annie and I were beginning anew.

All of our lives were changing. Marie, my elderly friend, came around to be with us. I was now living closer to her and she was delighted. We ordered in Chinese supper and put any thoughts of dramatic change away and ate heartily. We took a glass of champagne and celebrated the unknown.

Paul was next to move. He had planned to go to New Zealand with his cousin. I felt that it would be a marvellous experience and somehow thought that it would not be for long. Illusion! He has not returned as yet, eleven years on.

He was excited with the adventure. I met him in town some weeks before leaving. He was having difficulty with a very authoritarian colleague and he laughed as he said to me, "Two more weeks and I will see the end of her." I looked at him and thought her equivalent would be in Auckland to meet him.

My children laugh at my motives for learning a skill. "You might be stranded someday and you will need it," was my usual quote. I had a horrible feeling that when he got to New Zealand that if he did not know how to drive he would be left at the mercy of whoever would take him places. What if he wanted to go somewhere to clear his head? What if he just wanted to move away from it all? With that in mind I decided to teach him how to drive. My Honda Civic was not necessarily the easiest car to learn in. I decided to teach him in a local Business Park. At night time there is minimum traffic and you meet other learner drivers. I really enjoyed the privilege of teaching my son how to drive. Those moments were precious to me. The day I said to him that he was ready to drive on the main road so that he could catch the Luas, our local tram home, is etched in my memory. He drove flawlessly and parked perfectly. I felt a welling up of pride in him.

A few months later Paul left for New Zealand. I stood outside departures yet again and watched him go through. That cheeky chappy grin on his face as he was heading off into his life. I was going to miss him! "Honey, I'm home!" he would say when he came in the front door from school. I would never hear that again at least not in that context. He made me laugh. I experienced aliveness in his presence. His humour made the most difficult times bearable. That is some gift.

Interesting that when we change our perception, suddenly there is nothing to forgive. So long as we need someone to say sorry we are controlled by them.

> *Even though we announce to the world we are searching for answers to our mental and emotional states, all too often we really do not want to dig so deeply*

CHAPTER 27

Journey into Freedom

'The day you cease to travel; you will have arrived'

Japanese saying

WHEN walking in Tara many years ago the insight came to me that the answer to all of my difficulties lay in my response to the ordinary. That simple interpretation of the happenings of everyday living! Sometimes ordinary seems too ordinary and the desire is there in us all for the fantastic. Our tendency is to want lots of explanations, a touch of mystery, but this only serves to keep us far away from the truth. Truth is our mirror. It reflects the illusions, the beliefs, habits that have become our thought patterns. We know we are off centre when we are disturbed by life. Though disturbance seems a natural state because we all fall into that trap, it is not who we are.

Even though we announce to the world we are searching for answers to our mental and emotional states, all too often we really do not want to dig so deeply. It would mean we have to change our perception of life or what should be our life and change is not something we desire if it means taking us out of our comfort zone.

That programme that states that someone else is responsible for our happiness is too deeply engraved in our conscious minds. We have been programmed to blame others. This perception must change if we are to take more control of our lives. My desire for personal truth, to live a life of truth is what pushed me to make the changes in my life. There is no doubt that every so often I fall back into old habits especially when I am tired, but always that knowing is there, that through awareness I am responsible for my happiness, I am responsible for my thoughts, I am responsible for the reaction to my thoughts. This knowing is ever present and so it gives me a good kick in the butt.

My anger at life was not predominantly directed at others but at myself for making the choices that caused me unhappiness. Perception is very personal, based on our own experiences and over the years I evolved. Awareness is seeing without judgment, seeing leads to understanding and understanding leads to change if you choose to embrace it. Awareness is the letting go of attachment that life should be according to your perception. Who would want to live all of their lives limited to the perceptions created in our limited experience of life?

After Christmas Annie and I went to Japan to visit Grace. Annie feared flying and wondered if she could make the journey. I told her that she was not to worry and if she wanted she could stay at home with her sister Michelle. "And you would go without me?" she asked. I said, "Yes. I want you to come but if it is too much for you to face, then you are free to stay." Needless to say she came with me. We got as far as Amsterdam and the thought of the next twelve hours in the air was panicking her. I asked her a simple question. "Can you cope with the present moment; can you deal with whatever is happening to you right now?" She said she could. Then you will be fine on the journey so long as you keep this in mind.

The only thought that paralyses you is the one that says you can't live with the past or deal with the future. What is vitally important is that you always know that you can cope with the present. Flying into Narita airport she was cross that she could not see the end of the film she was watching. She had coped. Seeing Grace standing at a bus stop in Shinjuku lifted my spirits. Our children need to go beyond our boundaries.

Japan was not anything I was expecting. My thinking around it had more to do with the images of the Second World War and what I had witnessed on television. Getting off the bus and greeting Grace was to fundamentally change that perception of the Japanese people. She knew that I loved temples and took me to the most beautiful places. We went to Kamakura to visit the temples there and continued on to see the giant Daibutsu Buddha.

We also went to Nikko a small village that absolutely shattered my programmed perception of Japan.

Grace was aware that she needed to cater to the needs of a young teenager and took us on a ferry from Asakusa down the river to the monorail so that we could visit Odaiba. That was our shopping spree. While there Annie left her purse on a vending machine. We only noticed its absence when we got back to Grace's home. Grace told us to not to worry that this was Japan. Annie had all her savings in that purse and naturally she was apprehensive. It took us two train journeys to get back to the centre. Grace gave a description of the purse and the assistant went away and came back with it. Annie had left it on top of one of the machines. This, Grace said, is Japanese honour. You can expect your property to be respected.

Grace was working, so Annie and I decided to go to Ueno Zoo in search of Annie's passion, Pandas. We knew we had to take a few trains but as Grace had shown us the workings of the train station we felt we were all set to go. Six million people went through Shinjuku station each day. Whereas in India you felt every one of them, in Shinjuku you wondered where these people were. We were quite disappointed with the zoo and we made our way home. We took the same trains home but on the notice board on the train I saw a different terminal. I was not sure if we were on the right track and took out my dictionary and with what I thought was some clarity of questioning I spoke to a Japanese lady. She got up and left. I said to Annie, "So much for Japanese hospitality." Next I see her coming back with an exultant smile on her face. She poked me and poked the poor guy she had pulled over. He spoke English. We explained where we were going and he told us that this train normally went to our stop but today was one stop short. We needed to get on a different train. With that he spoke to this beautiful lady and she took care of us. She marched the pair of us off the train, took us across the platform and shouted Asagaya to us. We knew and understood. What a difference a day makes.

We just had to go to Tokyo Disney. I had never been to Disneyland so my senses got assailed. Whether I liked it or not, I went on all the various scary attractions. Being out of my comfort zone my intuition was failing me and while waiting to enter a roller coaster train I almost crushed some Japanese people who were exiting. Annie and Grace laughed uncontrollably. They could see the shocked faces of the people while I, like Magoo in the old cartoons, was blissfully unaware that what I was attempting to undertake was not possible. It didn't help that though I was only a size twelve and by Irish standards this is slim, by Japanese standards I was like a heifer! From my farming background that was not exactly the most flattering of descriptions. I was made aware of my shortcomings as most of the pillars on the streets were also mirrors.

The night before we left, Grace and I headed to a local children's park. We sat on the swings. We were not face to face so it was easier to talk. She poured out her heart to me and it was the greatest connection I had felt with her in a long time. It took moving very far away to give her that freedom to speak on what was important to her. Though I was yet again heartbroken seeing her standing on her own in Shinjuku at the bus stop where we met her, I felt that what was gained on this trip could never be lost.

Recently I met an old favourite TV personality Micheal O'Muircheartaigh in Tralee Co. Kerry. We spoke for a short time and he asked me if I had children. I told him that three of them had emigrated. In his deep Kerry accent, he asked, "And do you travel to them?" I said that I did. These characters had made me visit places that I never believed I would ever see. I can assure you Japan was not on my agenda ever and it was one of the most beautiful places I have ever visited. "There you go," he said. "They made you travel. Is that not a good thing?" There is no answer to truth.

I came home from Japan only to prepare for our final Chetana retreat at Sadhana Institute. Francis had completed his fourteen years there and was about to take a sabbatical at Notre Dame University, Indiana. This retreat was better than any that had gone before. The realisation that you do not have to do anything to attain spiritual freedom other than question your perceptions and beliefs, touched people. That we are loved beyond measure and we only have to realise it was clear to all of us present. The feeling of not being worthy has us in a bind.

Francis knew that he needed time out to explore his own feelings on where and what he wanted to do with the rest of his life. His desire to continue the work of Awareness unobstructed was predominant in his mind. He was beginning to feel the constraints of staying within the priesthood and needed time out to reflect. Though he had felt a need to be free for years the time seemed to be right for a move now.

While in Notre Dame we conducted retreats and it was wonderful. My work was too ordinary, too rooted in daily life for many of the participants who were for the most part psychologists. It is not easy to digest insight from someone not in their field. One told me that throughout my talks he wanted to go asleep and when it came to the meditation it gave him permission to sleep. I prayed for insight to his reaction and observed his behaviour in the group. He clearly had a problem with women so it was then easy to understand his attack on me. I put it to him this way. The Church and the most predominant religions are patriarchal. This has not brought the peace and oneness with God that the majority of people aspire to. I am the feminine approach. If you are only prepared to listen to the masculine, then you are seriously stuck. That which you are looking for will never be found so long as this is your perception. He did not reply.

An eminent psychologist Dr Thomas came to me and said "Liz, I know that you have not studied psychology but for every example you give I can put a clinical name to it. But I cannot do what you do, embodying this in ordinary living so, please do not change because you bring up uncomfortable feelings in others. What you are saying is coming from truth, and truth can stir. Please don't change!"

Francis came to a new freedom in America. He was happier than we had ever seen him. Away from Sadhana he had the time to reflect. He came back to Ireland to join me in a retreat in Dunderry Park, Co. Meath. This was a seven-day residential retreat in a beautiful setting and it was extremely beneficial to us all.

Michelle and James were getting married in a few weeks. When it comes to research and finding out what you want, Michelle is tops. She had her own ideas on what she wanted for her special day. I had said to her that when she had whittled down choices of dresses to the final five I would go with her. As she had many close friends as advisers and as they were of a different age group, I felt that maybe it might be right to step aside and not try to take over.

And so the day came when we went to choose a dress. I saw some that were really nice and spectacular but somehow I did not feel that they enhanced her strong presence. Michelle, I knew, could walk into a room and turn heads with her energy. You know she is around. Though she may not realise fully the powerfulness of that presence, it is there. So we came to dress number three. I took one look at her in it and wept. This dress was a significant statement. This was her!

Michelle had asked Francis to officiate at her wedding on August 1st. He was very happy to do this as they always had a lovely connection. The morning of the wedding was chaotic. Make-up artists and hairstylists took over. When Michelle put on her dress I had to stand back. Sarah, her friend took over. I needed to witness just how beautiful she looked but more than that, her very being was beautiful. She radiated happiness. McNabb, not to be left out, ran from room to room. The photographer, seeing this took what was the most wonderful photo of an animal who was more than a friend to every one of us.

It was a beautiful ceremony with readings that were in tune with this beautiful couple. The day had an essence to it that permeated the minds and hearts of all who attended. I had suggested that she invite people who had a heart connection to her and not to get caught up with pleasing everyone and everything. This was her special day.

The ceremony was in our local village church. It is the custom to have one of our local priests officiate too but he got ill and there was no replacement. Francis was on his own. The energy in the Church was beautiful. The music started as she walked down the aisle with her Dad and her bouquet of sunflowers. She got to the top of the church and waited. She turned around to me and said, "Do we have a priest?" I went to the sacristy and found Francis trying to find the proper garments. He had been abandoned by the sacristan who was meant to assist him. Lesson learned. Never pay the sacristan before the end of the ceremony!

Michelle and James were the next to leave Ireland. Michelle had won a trip around the world for two and planned to take a year off to explore. A long honeymoon! Their final destination was Melbourne. Sitting with them in their house prior to their departure I felt sad. Another ending, another new beginning! Looking at them move through the departure gate I felt at least they had each other. I felt the beginning stages of my shutting down though I did not fully understand it at the time.

Paul and Grace were home for her wedding. Grace, having completed her stay in Japan was heading to Melbourne too. I felt that life was moving far too quickly. Paul was to return to Auckland in October and Grace to Melbourne in November. I decided to have a family holiday on Achill, an island in the west of Ireland to experience the beauty of Ireland before they took off. At that time this visit had more to do with me than them. I wished for them to be anchored in what is wonderful about Ireland before they left. I really wanted them to wish to return. The trip wasn't a success in my mind because I was trying to recreate the past. On the way back I asked if they would like to visit Eddie and Annie Teresa in Sligo. All agreed they wanted to sit in that kitchen once more, smell the turf fire, eat Swiss roll and have tea. This was their childhood memory. I knocked on the door and Eddie opened it. His eyes welled up with tears when he saw who it was and he welcomed us with a welcome that no money on this earth can ever buy, as we all walked back in time to a memory of a much simpler life. "I thought I would never see you again" he said. Eddie and Annie Teresa connected them to their ancestors, to unconditional friendship and to the richness of a way of life that was dying in Ireland.

As small children Eddie brought them to work on the bog on the back of a tractor. They played in the fields with his daughter Aisling and got chased by a bull. She brought them to the railway line to place pennies on the track and they would return later to pick up the flattened pieces. Eddie taught Annie how to drive a tractor. They met terrifying countrified old ladies who would have had connections with their grandparents and great grandparents. When I think of integrity I think of Eddie and Annie Teresa. That wet, dreary, night the pack of cards came out and Grace and Paul were catapulted down memory lane to when Eddie taught them how to play Black Jack and Twenty-One. Then he rhymed off the riddles. Grace was in the best form I had seen her in years as she went head to head with Eddie on the riddles. We all had so much fun in his kitchen on that August evening that all of us found it difficult to leave because each one of us knew we might not all be together again in that house or experience the simplicity of love in that form for a long time to come. We all had to grow in our own individual ways.

Before Francis returned to America I took him to Glendalough, an ancient monastic site, to meditate. In the light of all the profound changes he had himself experienced in the previous several years he needed that to understand the direction of his life. He knew he had to live a life in truth. He could not continue to teach Awareness and remain ensconced within his comfort zone. I could not influence him one way or another. Decisions like these must emanate from one's own heart. I had enough experience in that area. Before we returned home that day, he came to a most important and difficult decision. He decided to leave the Jesuits whom he dearly loved without knowing what the next step was going to be. He returned home that day remarkably peaceful.

At the end of his stay at Notre Dame, he was keen on going back to live in India but he had no place to stay, no money to live on and no work to do. He was offered accommodation in Bombay by Sunil, his close friend and relative, to help him start out on his journey. No sooner had he arrived in Bombay than he contacted a virus that laid him low for weeks. No one near him to help him, he had to go through this process on his own. It is at times like this that your decisions are tested. Prior to this no matter what illness he experienced, he was in an organisation that provided the very best, now on his own in the world he was faced with the reality of life.

Life outside the Jesuits was difficult. Shorn of his previous identity and position, what he had to offer did not have the same value. Along with that came poverty. As he put it, he took a vow of poverty in the Jesuits but only when he left them did he experience poverty. After a life of service without financial considerations and without needing personal earning skills it was difficult to make the adjustment to having to fend for himself. But Francis was not without professional skills. He had lived in America for many years and had qualified as a clinical psychologist. He was Director of Sadhana Institute for fourteen years. He was acquainted with Anthony de Mello and had experienced the very best of teachers. You do not do all that and leave empty handed.

We continued to give retreats. This time it was different because while Francis was in the Jesuits, we had more invitations from religious orders. His leaving challenged their thinking. As he remained in the Jesuits we could get the viable numbers to conduct them, now that he had left it wasn't possible. Participants dropped by the wayside. We knew it would not be easy from now on but also knew that we had to live the message we taught. That was the challenge!

I returned to teaching to keep a steady income flowing. The seminars and workshops were not enough to keep Annie and me afloat and Francis had to begin all over again. A spirituality that is not practical is in the clouds. My old school needed a substitute and I availed of the offer for three weeks. That few weeks then developed into more. I realised just how much I missed working with children. Some were not the easiest to handle but the more I worked with them the more I connected to them and became alive. The moment you work with difficult children you see more than their difficulties. You begin to see the child behind the behaviour. Once that happens everything changes.

One Christmas we had a talent show. High up in the charts was Shane Ward's song "That's my Goal" They loved it. My goal was to get them to sing their hearts out but no matter how much we practised one or other would start a fight. On the day, I don't know what was more beautiful, their singing or their trust in me. They rose to the occasion. We reached our goal. They didn't need to win. No one could take that experience from them.

I needed to be emotionally strong enough to maintain a loving structure for them. I could have kept a controlled structure and a distance from them but that would not have benefited them. Within the structure they had to experience being loved.

Barry was my challenge. He couldn't stay still and was always swinging on the chair because of his ADHD diagnosis. He had also gained a reputation and this did not make it easy for him or me. He talked non-stop, distracted every other child, passed inappropriate comments and swung on that chair. You might get the impression he wasn't listening but later he would ask the most poignant questions.

The local priest decided to pay a visit. He thought in his innocence to speak about God. Who is God? Basically, what did God look like to them? He was met with silence. He moved from

God to Jesus. Perhaps he would have more success. How did we know there was ever a Jesus? More silence! He mentioned some famous people. Silence! Eventually he mentioned Napoleon and one bright spark said he knew him. How do you know him? "In a book," came the reply. So he declared, "In a book! That is how we know about Jesus." Barry swung over and back. He was also eating his lunch. He didn't like being interrupted eating his breakfast roll. I looked at the glint in his eye as he weighed up the question and waited for the arrow to find its target. He began slowly, "I could say Joseph – his friend across the table - was gay, in a book, three hundred years ago." Poor Joseph got such a fright he declared, "I'm not f++++g gay." Barry thought for a second and said, "And it could all be lies. How do we know there was ever a Jesus then?"

The poor priest was no match for this and told him not to say another word until he had eaten his lunch. He was safe enough as it would take Barry some time to finish it. He got his point across that questions were not welcome especially questions that challenged this man's beliefs.

That moment I saw how important it is to have the freedom to question, but to be able to question appropriately you also need someone who is able to receive the question without strong reactions. I avoided questioning as a child and continued with this interpretation right up into my adult life. In short I was remaining infantile. I too learned a powerful lesson that day.

The next generation will question and we need to grow up to be ready for answers, and also to have the maturity to acknowledge that sometimes we do not have answers. This child pushed me to live a life of truth. There is no question that many of his behaviours were out of order. These were skills that needed to be learned. He also challenged me to find the courage to be a voice for him. I learned a lot in that year.

Every three months Francis had to return to India or visit America due to visa restrictions. We worked well together and throughout that time I needed to revisit my attitudes to relationships. I realised that I was wary of losing my freedom. I had to unlock my underlying fear and what it amounted to was that I did not trust me to make correct decisions around men. I feared getting attached, becoming dependent again. I feared slipping back to old ways and habits of putting my needs last on the list, especially around strong male authority figures and Francis was strong.

I had never envisaged getting married again, seeing my children and my work as being sufficient yet this gentle blending of two hearts happened so effortlessly and in Clonmacnoise an ancient monastic site, down by the River Shannon on a beautiful evening we decided to get married. Love could only happen when I knew the truth about myself and when I understood that I could trust myself not to go into the shadow again. Only when I laid my fears to rest, and let go of my sadness could my heart be ready to open to love again. "When the heart is unobstructed the result is love." (Chuang Tzu)

Living an aware life was the way to go. Only awareness could protect me from reverting into old ways and I needed to be mindful of that.

Life happens! Reality, what is before us is not the problem, our response to it is. That response will determine our state of mind, our peace. We need to Wake Up!

The difference between now and 1996 is my experience of life. People who used to upset me and the situations that crippled me, no longer have that power. You could say it is because I have gotten older but I know it is much more than that. It is the total immersion in the experience that is different.

Recently I was sitting among the children in the classroom working with clay. All were working away happily when one little girl began to sing a hymn I taught them.

The refrain goes

"It's a story about love,
It's a parable of love that Jesus told."

Life is about love, being able to love. So long as we hold on to hurt feelings we limit our availability either to receive or give love. That is truth!

When the eye is unobstructed the result is sight,
When the ear is unobstructed the result is hearing,
When the mind is unobstructed the result is truth,
When the heart is unobstructed the result is joy and
love. Chuang Tsu.